Managing Training

To Jacqueline

I hope you
enjoy it!

Best regards,

Sunny

The Kogan Page Practical Trainer Series

Series Editor: Roger Buckley

PRACTICAL  TRAINER SERIES

Managing Training

SUNNY STOUT

KOGAN PAGE
Published in association with the
Institute of Training and Development

With thanks to Jan Duncan-John

First published in 1993

Kogan Page Limited
120 Pentonville Road
London N1 9JN

© Sunny Stout, 1993

British Library Cataloguing in Publication Data

A CIP record for this book is available from the British Library.

ISBN 0 7494 0838 3

Typeset by Witwell Ltd, Southport
Printed and bound in Great Britain by Biddles Ltd, Guildford and King's Lynn

Contents

PART IV EXTERNAL TRAINING CONSULTANTS

PART V PROMOTING TRAINING IN YOUR ORGANIZATION

Series Editor's Foreword

Organizations get things done when people do their jobs effectively. To make this happen they need to be well trained. A number of people are likely to be involved in this training: identifying the needs of the organization and of the individual, selecting or designing appropriate training to meet those needs, delivering it and assessing how effective it was. It is not only 'professional' or full-time trainers who are involved in this process; personnel managers, line managers, supervisors and job holders are all likely to have a part to play.

This series has been written for all those who get involved with training in some way or another, whether they are senior personnel managers trying to link the goals of the organization with training needs or job holders who have been given responsiblity for training newcomers. Therefore, the series is essentially a practical one which focuses on specific aspects of the training function. This is not to say that the theoretical underpinnings of the practical aspects of training are unimportant. Anyone seriously interested in training is strongly encouraged to look beyond 'what to do' and 'how to do it' and to delve into the areas of why things are done in a particular way.

The series has become so popular that it is intended to include additional volumes whenever a need is found for practical guidelines in some area of training.

The authors have been selected because they have considerable practical experience. All have shared, at some time, the same difficulties, frustrations and satisfactions of being involved in training and are now in a position to share with others some helpful and practical guidelines.

In this book Sunny Stout tackles the difficult area of managing training. There are many people who become managers of training departments or sections who have little, if any, experience of training. The false idea is often expressed that one doesn't necessarily need to know anything about training to manage the function. It is also something of a false assumption that specialist trainers are able, as a matter of course, to be able to manage training without any further development of their knowledge and skills.

In reality nothing is further from the truth. A training manager must have credibility in the eyes of the training team as someone who knows about training and in the eyes of the organization as someone who understands the business.

In those organizations where training still has a low profile, training managers need to market the expertise of their team and to get closer to the hub of activity where they can be seen to be contributing to the achievement of organisational goals through the medium of human resources. In those organisations where the profile is high, the training manager will be expected to meet the demands of an executive team who will be aware of what the training department should be contributing to the organizations and who intend to exploit it to the full.

It is difficult to be prescriptive in deciding how training managers should be trained and in what. This book covers the major activities in which all training managers are likely to be involved, and serves as a valuable guide to those who have been doing the job for some time, as well as to those who are new and still trying to identify their role.

ROGER BUCKLEY

Introduction

Managing Training clarifies the need for training, and demystifies the management of training within your organization. In today's social and economic climate more organizations have begun to focus on training as a central management function. There is an urgent need for competent, trained staff within every organization. This is due to discerning and knowledgeable customers, fast advances in technology and changing social attitudes.

Why Manage Training?

Competent, trained staff can only emerge if the correct training is available. The correct training benefits individual staff from the top to the bottom and is invaluable to all organizations. Training is an investment in the people who work with and for you, and an investment in people is the best investment your organization can make.

No matter what size your organization is at present, you will benefit from understanding exactly what specific training can do for you. By improving employee knowledge, skills and behaviour, performance will be enhanced, productivity will be increased and profits will be multiplied.

What Will You Gain?

This is a practical handbook on managing training within an organization – be it in the commercial, education, industrial or public sector. This handbook will help you to:

1. Clarify the role and function of the training department within your particular organization.
2. Evaluate the effectiveness of your training team and training facilities, and to consider how to select new trainers for your team if they are necessary.
3. Calculate a return on training, including the validation and evaluation of your organization's training activities.
4. Decide if you need an external training consultancy. How to select an external training consultancy, and brief the trainers and assess their programmes.
5. Promote the benefits of training within your organization, build up commitment, and combat negative attitudes to training.

How to Use this Book

Managing Training offers a practical, hands-on guide for the busy executive to develop training within the organization. This handbook will take you through the training jungle. It can be worked on to suit your needs – at any time and at any pace.

- **Part I Managing the Training Department:** identifies the key points for you to consider in managing training. The five chapters are to help clarify the role and function of the training department within your organization.
- **Part II Managing the Training Team:** helps you evaluate the effectiveness of your training team and training facilities; looks at the importance of gaining feedback from trainers and trainees; and considers how to select new trainers for your team.
- **Part III Your Training Budget – The Financial Return:** investigates how to calculate a return on training – one of the fundamental areas to be managed as head of the training function. A systematic approach to training includes validation and evaluation of an organization's training activities.
- **Part IV External Training Consultants:** considers why your organization may choose to select an external training consultancy. The four chapters examine the selection process, how to brief the external consultant, what criteria are expected from an external trainer, and what courses are available.
- **Part V Promoting Training in Your Organization:** highlights the importance of the performance appraisal and its link to

training, and identifies the necessary skills and methods to promote the value and benefits of training within your organization.

Each chapter follows a similar layout:

- **Summary** – Every chapter begins with a brief summary of the key topics to be discussed.
- **Trainer's Tips** – Practical advice and assistance is offered in helpful tips and techniques.
- **Checklists** – Several chapters have checklists. These are a source of reference which provide a practical approach to many different training situations.
- **Examples** – Real training problems and their solutions are summarized to help you with your own training decisions.
- **Conclusion & Chapter Review** – Each chapter ends with a conclusion and review to highlight main chapter topics.

1 The Role of Training

▷   **CHAPTER SUMMARY**   ◁

This chapter examines where and how to begin as head of the training function within your organization.

- Where do you begin?
- Your role as head of training
- Where training fits into the organization

Where Do You Begin?

Where should you begin as head of the training function? It is important to identify what your role is as head of training, and to identify where training fits into the organizational structure.

All employees have training needs at different stages in their careers. Four basic needs are:

- Company and product induction for new recruits
- Acquisition of basic job skills
- Development of new knowledge, skills and attitudes
- Assistance in adjusting to retirement or redundancy

Training in the private or public sector includes formal training on courses designed and delivered by in-company trainers, external consultants, or a combination of both.

Your role will be that of managing the training function whether you employ in-house or external trainers. For the purpose of this book we will refer to in-house trainers as internal trainers.

What is Your Role as Head of Training?

One of the first areas to consider are your terms of reference: where do you fit in the structure of the organization? To clarify this you need to answer two questions:

1. What is your position within the organization?
   - Senior Manager?
   - Line Manager?
   - Staff Manager?
2. Where are you placed on the organization tree?
   - What are your reporting lines?
   - What is your power base?

Trainer's Tip

Terms of reference identify:
- What has to be done in terms of training?
- Whose responsibility is the training function? (eg line management and training management)
- Who is committed to and owns the training programmes? (eg line managers, trainers or trainees)

---

1 *What is your position within the organization?*

Senior Management: If you are a manager at the most senior level within your organization, you will be directly involved in the running of the company with responsibility for the most effective use of resources, both capital and personnel.

A senior manager, responsible for policy and strategic decisions at top level, is instrumental in the planning and development of managers and staff.

As head of training at senior level you will be directly accountable for overseeing the training function.

Line Management: The chain of command within your organization will tell you whether you are a line manager or a staff manager. In line management, there is a clear chain of command which directly links senior managers and line managers.

Typically, the line manager has control over a number of staff and is responsible for a key operating department. For example, as a line manager who is head of the training function you may be responsible for training, or even personnel and training.

Staff Management: On the other hand, you may fulfil the role of staff manager. A staff manager has responsibility over a number of staff, but

Figure 1.1 *Management matrix*

is not responsible for the main operating activities of the organization. Instead, staff management provides line management with support or advisory services. See Figure 1.1.

As a staff manager you may be entitled 'Training Manager', but your role will be different from that of a line manager. You will most likely be responsible to a line manager who is head of Human Resources, or Personnel & Training. Part of your overall job description may include the role of full-time trainer.

2 *Where are you placed on the organization tree?*

Organization Tree: Whatever your role, an organization tree (or chart) will clearly denote where you are positioned in the company, and help to explain what are the reporting lines in your organization.

The organization tree is a graphic representation of the formal relationship between functions, jobs and people in the company.

Line or executive responsibility can be indicated by linking jobs with continuous lines, while staff or advisory relationships are indicated with dotted lines; see eg Figure 1.2.

Reporting Lines: Once you know where you are placed on the organization tree, you can begin to look at the reporting lines within

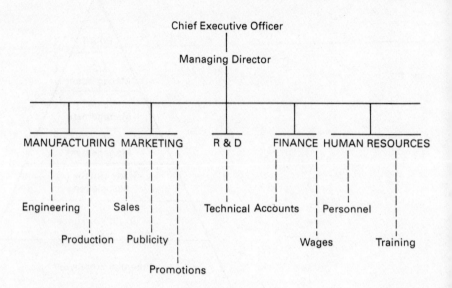

Figure 1.2 *Organization tree*

the organization. Your reporting responsibility is determined by several factors:

1. To whom do you report?
2. Who reports to you?
3. What is your power base?

These three questions will help you analyse how to ensure your voice is heard. It also makes clear how many people you should consult each time you plan to implement new strategies, institute change, or delegate a task or project.

> **Trainer's Tip**
> The key to the power which you hold as head of training is determined by the value that the organization places on the training function. Power is related to the resources which you manage as head of training.

Power Base: An integral aspect in defining your power base is to

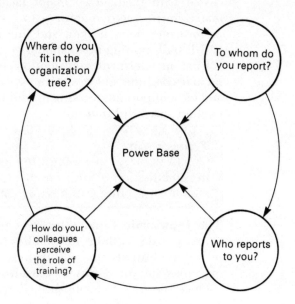

Figure 1.3 *Power base*

understand how your colleagues see the training function. Figure 1.3 illustrates the elements which influence your power base.

Many line managers perceive themselves as having no responsibility or link to the training function. Managers with this philosophy tend to expect the training manager to shoulder most training activities. These may include an analysis of training needs, setting objectives, designing and implementing training programmes, and monitoring the effectiveness of training carried out.

If line managers lack commitment, the training manager shoulders a double burden: enlisting support and participation for all facets of training as well as managing the training activities. However, if line managers are involved at every step, it establishes ownership and commitment to the training function.

In an ideal world line managers are responsible for the training of their staff, and your role as head of training is to educate line management in their responsibilities. This is because accountability for employee training should ultimately rest with the line manager or supervisor.

Line managers may need encouragement to be involved in the

training process, and therefore all training activities should be discussed with them. Two major factors for consideration are: line management accountability to senior management for the performance of their staff, and line management's ability to assess which staff training needs should be met.

Line management contribution to the training function may include coaching and developing staff; analysing staff training needs; and most important, working in conjunction with the head of training to effect successful training.

> **Trainer's Tip**
> One of the ways to establish the significance of training within the organization is to ensure that line managers are aware of the relevance of training in meeting corporate objectives.

The Diplomatic Link: Whichever role you perform, one of your primary tasks will be to establish a rapport with line and staff managers. Initially this will include a clarification of their training objectives and the results expected from training.

Once the link is established, it will be easier to encourage line managers to participate in the training process. To develop this link, and rapport, two questions should be examined:

1. What is the attitude to the training function in your company?
2. Have previous trainers failed to achieve set objectives?

> **Trainer's Tip**
> Developing a liaison between training and line management is essentially an exercise in diplomacy – ie a planned and continuous effort to maintain understanding and to communicate effectively with the people concerned. These are all those line managers, with whom you need to work, who require a structured approach to staff training.

Example

Recently, in a large mail-order company, the head of training spent a day with each of nine divisional managers. The objective was to clarify how they saw the way forward in terms of skills and management training.

The end result of this diplomacy was excellent. Relations were

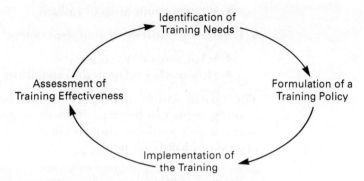

Figure 1.4 *The training function*

improved between the training department and line management, encouraging trust on both sides and management participation in the training function.

An action plan was devised to push forward plans for individual coaching, group skills training, and a new management development programme for personnel in each of the nine divisions.

Where Training Fits into the Organization

Success in training depends on a systematic approach. Before this is possible it is vital to learn where training fits into the structure of your organization. Normally, the training department is responsible for the training function. The four main stages of the training function are:

1. Identification and analysis of training needs
2. Formulation of a training policy
3. Implementation of the training
4. Assessment of training effectiveness

The interrelationship of these four factors is shown in Figure 1.4.

To fulfil the training function within your organization the following criteria need to be evaluated. They relate specifically to managing the training department.

- What is the capacity of your department?
- What are your responsibilities as head of training?
- What are the individual positions and responsibilities of your staff?

- What are your areas of influence?
- *What is the capacity of your department?*
  - What needs can you meet?
  - How do they relate to the capabilities within your department?

The capacity within your department will help you to determine what training needs can be met within the organization. The number of training staff available also determines who is to be involved in the process of identifying needs.

> **Trainer's Tip**
> A comprehensive analysis of training needs (known as TNA – training needs analysis) within an organization takes into account:
> - Corporate objectives
> - Job descriptions and job specifications
> - Employee knowledge, skills, and attitudes
> - Cost of inadequate job performance
> - Training resources

It is likely that there are possibilities for developing expertise within the training department. If you manage a small team, or are on your own, it may be necessary to look outside the organization for assistance.

- *What are your responsibilities as head of training?*

As head of training are you a senior manager, line manager or staff manager? This will influence what say you have in managing the training function.

Who is responsible for determining training priorities and implementing the overall view of training? If you report to a senior manager responsible for implementing training strategies and policies, what is your role?

Example
A UK company who manufacture and distribute cardboard corrugated cases recruited a training manager with responsibilites for staff training. Her key duties were listed in a job description as follows:

- To identify staff training needs in all departments
- To prepare training plans as required

- To design and implement training programmes
- To measure and analyse results

This particular manager was not responsible for management training in any capacity. Within one year, she realized that line management required specific training to ensure the success of her staff training programmes. As a result, she put forward a proposal analysing the reasons why line management needed training and how this would support the existing training process.

- *What are the individual positions and responsibilities of your staff?* What involvement do your staff have in the training process? Are they primarily trainers who implement training programmes? Or are they accountable for the selection, design and production of training programmes?

Person specification: To understand and maintain control over the specific roles of your staff, each member should have a person specification which briefly summarizes each individual trainer's knowledge, skills, past experience and personal characteristics. This should be in addition to a job description and job specification.

Job description: A job description provides a basic framework for the trainer's job, and outlines the key purpose, duties and responsibilities of the job.

Job specification: A job specification outlines the physical and mental activities demanded from the job. Essential characteristics of the job holder are outlined according to required knowledge, skills and attitudes. This can include the qualifications, experience and personal qualities required to perform the job.

- *What are your areas of influence?*

In your training capacity you are a motivating force, influencing the scope of training within the organization. Two major areas of influence are:

1. What direction training may take within the organization
2. How training develops in relation to training needs and objectives

Trainer's Tip – Areas of influence
It is critical that you understand what senior management's attitude is to the training function in your organization. From your position and power base, you can determine how, why and

whether you are able to influence important decisions which affect training policies and strategy.

Conclusion

In this chapter we have surveyed where to begin as head of the training function within your organization. First determine what your position is within the organization; and second identify where training fits into the overall structure of the company.

▶ **CHAPTER REVIEW** ◀

- To begin as head of the training function it is important to identify two factors:
    1. Your role as head of training
    2. Where training fits into the organization
- To establish your terms of reference:
    1. What is your position within the company?
    2. Where are you placed on the organization tree?
- Your reporting responsibility is determined by:
    1. Whom do you report to?
    2. Who reports to you?
    3. What is your power base?
- Where training fits into the organization depends on a structured approach:
    1. Identification of training needs
    2. Formulation of a training policy
    3. Implementation of the training
    4. Assessment of training effectiveness
- To fulfil the role of the training department within the organization evaluate:
    1. What is the capacity of your department?
    2. What are your responsibilities as head of training?
    3. What are the positions and individual responsibilities of your staff?
    4. What are your areas of influence?

2 Training Missions and Objectives

▷   CHAPTER SUMMARY   ◁

How corporate objectives and training objectives reflect the corporate mission and the training mission.
- The corporate mission
- The training mission
- Corporate objectives
- Training objectives

The Corporate Mission

In recent years it has become fashionable for companies to define their business in one statement. This includes their business aims, who their customers are, what their products and services are, and what distinguishes their business in terms of cost, quality, reliability and value for money. This is called the mission statement.

Within your organization there should be an overall mission statement whose philosophy is carried out departmentally. The mission statement of an organization states the basic purpose of an organization or its higher goals.

How to write a mission statement

Because your mission states the broad purpose of your company, it indicates the direction in which you are heading. A complete mission statement includes three items:

1. The organization's basic products/services
2. The functions to be performed
3. The markets to be served

Examples of mission statements

The company mission statement may be similar to one of the following:

'To distribute high quality electronic components throughout the UK.'

'To provide our European business clients with solutions to working more efficiently.'

'To supply quality food provisions at competitive prices to all our customers.'

The Training Mission

The training mission indicates the higher goals of the training department and should reflect the corporate mission. In fact, it is necessary for training objectives, policies and strategies to mirror corporate objectives, policies and strategies.

If you have yet to devise a training mission, you may like to consider the examples below. Remember that the training mission, unlike objectives, cannot be measured.

Examples of Training Missions

'To provide training to meet the highest quality needs for staff and ultimately for customers.'

'The training department will provide a wide variety of training services to suit the needs of all staff and departments within the organization.'

'The training department will supervise the design and implementation of training programmes to satisfy the training needs of staff and management for all UK branches.'

Corporate Objectives

Because the corporate mission statement denotes the organization's overall purpose, it follows that corporate objectives will reflect these higher goals and indicate how they are to be achieved. The next step is to examine these corporate objectives to define objectives for the training department.

Definition: Corporate objectives are quite simply objectives which reflect corporate philosophy. These are usually measurable short-term and long-term objectives which comprise the total range of a company's activities. To increase market share or profitability is an objective.

Ideally, every department is involved in setting these goals as they will contribute to organizational or corporate success.

Example
The objectives for a manufacturing company could be:
> Our corporate objectives for next year are to:
> - Increase sales revenue by 15 per cent
> - Achieve a profit of £20 million
> - Maintain a market share of 22 per cent of the UK market for our products

Trainer's Tip
Training managers are often in a key position to influence the objectives set by an organization. Objectives are concrete and measurable business goals. They are generally set out as performance targets in areas such as sales, market share, production or profitability.

Corporate objectives are specific targets that support your organization's survival, and there is generally a set period of time in which to achieve them. This should be reflected in the organization's one year, three year and five year business plans.

Corporate objectives are primary objectives and relate to the organization's principal business. None the less, each department will ultimately be responsible for devising departmental strategies and plans to implement these objectives.

Training Objectives

As training is essentially a service function, it must support senior management in meeting corporate objectives. Training objectives state

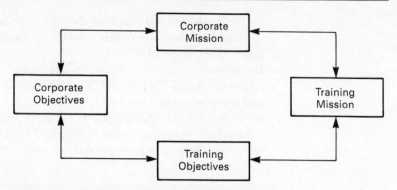

Figure 2.1 *Linking missions and objectives*

the objectives of the training process and indicate how the training mission is to be achieved. Training objectives, unlike the training mission, can be quantified.

One of your first tasks, as head of training, is to ask who is responsible for outlining corporate objectives. Corporate objectives are normally set by the senior management team. However, there should be input from all the principal departments concerned.

Your second task will be to determine who is responsible for setting, monitoring and meeting organizational training objectives. Organizational training objectives not only complement corporate objectives; they provide a focus for the actions of the training department. Figure 2.1 highlights the link between missions and objectives.

Training objectives are precise goals and can be measured. They will define the precise targets of the training function, and can be set for:

- the organization
- an individual department or division
- individual training programmes
- individual trainees

This is because training objectives refer to change, change that will affect a trainee's performance or behaviour. For example, a training objective may be expressed as follows:

Examples of organizational training objectives
'To increase productivity and efficiency of all skilled staff through training.'

'To ensure all managers are trained in the necessary management techniques to improve task delegation and improve time-management skills.'

'To provide full product training for all newly recruited staff, with refresher courses at required intervals.'

It may be that within your organization all training activity is an integral part of the personnel function. What is important is that you are involved in the process of setting training objectives.

The following checklist and activity will help you to define your training mission and training objectives.

CHECKLIST

1. What is your corporate mission statement?
2. Is there any evidence within the organization that this mission is adhered to?
3. Do you know exactly what your organization's corporate objectives are?
4. Do you have access to the company business plans, and how often are they reviewed and updated?
5. Is training an integral part of this?

Activity

Equipped with your corporate mission statement and corporate objectives, devise an appropriate:

- training mission statement;
- statement of training objectives.

Remember that your training mission and training objectives will reflect your corporate mission and organizational objectives.

Conclusion

- The corporate mission is the organization's higher goals. Corporate objectives explain how the corporate mission will be achieved.
- The training mission indicates the overall purpose of the training department and reflects the corporate mission.

- Training objectives indicate how the training mission will be accomplished and complement corporate objectives. All objectives can be measured or quantified.

▶ **CHAPTER REVIEW** ◀

1. The corporate mission statement
A mission statement is stated simply in one sentence or paragraph and contains three basic factors:
1. Basic products/services
2. Functions to be performed
3. The markets to be served

2. The training mission statement
The philosophy of your training department will reflect the corporate mission statement. This simple statement should be in harmony with senior management or organizational ethos.

3. Corporate objectives
Corporate objectives are targets set to reflect corporate or organizational philosophy. They are usually set by the senior management team and can be measured.

4. Training objectives
Training objectives can be set once corporate objectives are defined.

3 Training Policies

▷   CHAPTER SUMMARY   ◁

In this chapter we discuss the basics of designing a training policy.
- What is a training policy?
- Brief policy statements
- The longer policy statement
- The focus of training activities

What is a Training Policy?

Having determined your organizational training objectives, you are ready to move on to develop training policies and strategies.

Policies play a major role in the planning activities of any organization and function as a framework for management to achieve corporate objectives.

A business policy states how an organization intends to accomplish its objectives. A training policy not only states how training will achieve its set objectives, but also spells out the focus of training activities within the organization. Figure 3.1 illustrates the process of setting training policies.

The policy should clearly state that all employees be trained and developed to the maximum of their potential and ability in relation to corporate objectives. It will indicate which staff are to be trained and why, and how that training will be implemented.

Although it is vital that all management and staff support the organization's training policy, it is even more important that training

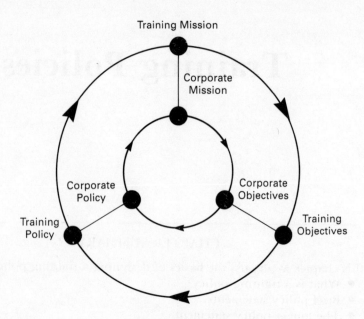

Figure 3.1 *The process of setting training policies*

is seen and valued by all employees as an opportunity to develop their know-how, skill and proficiency.

The three key components of a training policy are:

1. The training mission
   (the training philosophy or higher goals of the training department)
2. The training objectives
   (the specific targets set to fulfil the organization's training mission)
3. The training procedures
   (how the training objectives are to be implemented)

The training policy gives every individual within an organization the opportunity to develop their knowledge, skills and expertise for the good of the company.

Whether the personnel and training functions are combined or separate in your organization, the training policy will state precisely what the organization is prepared to do to develop employee potential.

Brief Policy Statements

In some organizations the policy is a simple statement combining the corporate training mission and the organization's training objectives (see the examples below).

Examples

- The company will provide the resources and support necessary to ensure that all staff and management are well trained in the fundamental tasks required to accomplish their job efficiently and satisfactorily in pursuit of specific corporate goals.
- All employees will be given support and guidance to maximize performance in line with specific corporate targets.
- Training will be made available to all members of staff who will be consulted and asked to participate in training and development programmes to master their primary job responsibilities and support the organization's key business goals.

Trainer's Tip
Will you be responsible for setting training priorities?
Your overall objective as head of training is to ensure that the trainers in your team acquire the skills and behaviour which will guarantee that training objectives (organizational, departmental and individual) can be achieved, and training policies fulfilled effectively and efficiently.

The Longer Policy Statement

A longer policy statement incorporates details on how organizational training objectives are to be implemented. The policy must be included within the organization's annual business plan or the company's personnel policy. A comprehensive policy statement, which includes the three key components, may look similar to the example cited below.

A Training Policy

The Training Mission
It is in the interest of the organization and all its employees that full support be given to training and development.

Training Objectives

1. The primary objective of the organization's training and development programme will be to support the achievement of corporate objectives in line with the business plan.

2. The training department will provide a wide variety of training services to satisfy the needs of all staff and management within the organization.

Training Procedures

1. Training objectives will be agreed with all supervisors and managers concerned with staff training.

2. Training needs will be systematically identified before any training is selected.

3. When a training need has been identified, specific to an employee's job performance or behaviour, all employees and their immediate managers will be consulted prior to implementation of any training.

4. A training plan will be designed, setting out training procedures relevant to employee training needs, and with particular reference to certain requirements in the organization's business plan.

5. A list of the training staff who will be responsible for designing, delivering and evaluating the training programmes will be published on a regular basis.

6. External consultants may be used where required if an internal trainer is not available to run the required programme.

7. Induction training and job training will be made available to all new employees, whether staff or management, full or part-time.

8. Opportunities will be made for selected employees preparing for a new job role to participate in training when necessary.

9. All training and development activities, whether internal programmes or those provided by an external consultancy, are to be assessed and evaluated regularly.

10. The organization's training policy will be reviewed on an annual basis in accordance with the business plan.

The Focus of Training Activities

Within your organization it is important for you to determine whether training will focus on immediate learning needs which are related to present job tasks, or whether training and development will be linked closely to your organization's short, medium and long-term business plans.

The longer-term view will have a greater effect on the organization's ability to deal with customers and meet customer needs. A more far-reaching training policy will also be strategically linked to the organization's marketing and strategic plans.

Your training policy will be determined initially by the corporate mission (or higher goals) of your organization. It is essential that your training policy be supportive of corporate objectives and policies.

Trainer's Tip
The objective of a marketing strategy is to decide how to maintain intelligence about the market-place through marketing research, how to identify and reach customers, and how to secure sales and generate a profit.

Activity
1. Is there a corporate training policy already in existence in your organization?
2. Does this training policy reflect the role of the training department as a support in achieving corporate objectives?
3. Where does this policy fit into the company's one year, three year, and five year business plans (or short, medium and long-term plans)?
4. Can you break the current policy down into the three key components: the training mission, the training objectives, and the training procedures?

Conclusion

In this chapter we have examined the basics for drawing up a training policy. Training policies and strategies can be developed once organizational training objectives have been set.

CHAPTER REVIEW

1. Training Policy
A training policy states how training will achieve its set objectives, and spells out the focus of training activities within the organization.
2. The key components of a training policy are:
    1. The training mission
    2. The training objectives
    3. Training procedures
3. Brief policy statement
Simply combines the corporate training mission and training objectives.
4. Longer policy statement
Incorporates training procedures at some length. In other words it details how the training objectives are to be implemented.
5. The focus of training activities
Training and development activities should be closely linked to the organization's short, medium, and long-term business plans.

4 Training Strategies

┌───┐

▷   CHAPTER SUMMARY   ◁

Training strategy is the campaign to implement training policies in order to achieve corporate objectives.

- What is a training strategy?
- Implementation of training strategies
- The SWOT Analysis

└───┘

Definition of strategy

Before we can identify what comprises a training strategy, it is important to understand the term strategy itself.

Although originally a military term, strategy has come to be linked to the process of planning and preparation in business or any organization. Within an organization, a strategy is the catalyst to implement policies.

What is a Training Strategy?

A training strategy outlines, in broad terms, the campaign for the training function. It is a statement of intent which:

- Provides the basis for the implementation of training policies
- Outlines the course of action designed to achieve training objectives

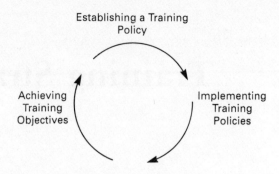

Figure 4.1 *Implementing the training strategy*

Training as an agent of change

In any organization, the major purpose of training is to achieve performance from staff and management. Training is often described as a 'change agent', which means that its primary purpose is to effect change in employee knowledge, skills performance or behaviour.

This is where training is different from education. As Buckley and Caple (1990) note, education is person-oriented and training is job-oriented. Education is concerned with the development of the individual. The aims of education are to provide that individual with an understanding of a subject which can be interpreted and applied according to individual situations or circumstances.

Training, on the other hand, is concerned with development of the individual for the ultimate good of the organization in achieving its goals and targets.

Implementation of Training Strategies

Your training strategy will revolve around three key factors (see Figure 4.1):

1. Establishing a training policy (which we examined in Chapter 3)
2. Implementing the training policy
3. Achieving organizational training objectives

However, to be properly effective, a training strategy must take into account the various elements which affect the organization. For example, corporate policies, corporate culture, the working environment, the external market-place and the community environment. These are only a few of the factors which can influence the training function. A more comprehensive list of items is offered below. What other factors can you add to this list?

- Management policies and style
- Organizational culture
- Business plans (short-, medium-, long-term)
- The working environment
- The market-place (new customers and markets)
- The size of your training department
- The expertise of your trainers
- Current training programmes and products
- The training budget
- New materials required
- Nature of the jobs within the organization
- Motivation and morale of the workforce
- The local community and environment

> **Trainer's Tip**
> Strategic planning is a management process in which you may be involved in your role as head of training. Corporate planning takes into consideration the market environment, current trends and fashions, the development of new products or services, and new areas of business.
> In practical terms, your training strategy will match the short-term, medium-term and long-term plans of your organization. This will involve an assessment of internal strengths and weaknesses, and external opportunities and threats (see Figure 4.2). Once this assessment is complete, an evaluation of alternative strategies may be required.

The SWOT Analysis

> **Activity**
> In order to devise your training strategy, it is vital to determine the strengths, weaknesses, opportunities and threats which affect the training environment.
> a. Devise your own list of influential factors, taking into account

S Strengths	W Weaknesses
O Opportunities	T Threats

Figure 4.2 *The SWOT analysis*

all the items listed above. Once you have your final list, divide it into positive and negative influences.

b. Now you are ready to produce your SWOT analysis. Most likely the majority of positive influences will end up in the STRENGTHS box, and the negatives will be divided among WEAKNESSES, OPPORTUNITIES and THREATS.

c. Having completed your SWOT analysis, answer the following questions:

1. What new factors need to be taken into consideration for this planning year?

2. What changes would you recommend to your current training strategy?

3. What needs to be done to implement current strategies?

A checklist will help you identify what your role will be in planning training strategy.

CHECKLIST

1. How involved will you be in the planning stages?

  • This involves planning for short-, medium- and long-term strategies.

  • What knowledge and skills will you require if you are to be involved in forecasting, budgeting and costing?

2. Will you be responsible for setting training priorities?

  • Remember that the overall objective of trainers is to help the trainee to acquire the behaviour which will give the most effective work performance and help to achieve organizational objectives.

---

3. Who else is involved in setting training policy and strategy?
   - Who will be involved in the planning meetings?
   - What will be your role?
4. What new planning is required?
   - Will you be responsible for making specific proposals?
   - Who else will be involved?
5. What steps need to be taken to implement current strategies?
   - Who implemented strategies before you?
   - Where do you fit in?
   - What steps do you need to take to implement current strategies?

Trainer's Tip
Remember, for strategic planning to be successful, teamwork and co-operation are required.

Strategic course of action

The next step is to outline the course of action which translates your training strategy into tactics. This course of action is your training plan.

The training plan provides for the selection, design and implementation of your training programmes. This will be covered in detail in Chapter 5.

Conclusion

In this chapter we defined training strategy as the campaign to implement training policies in order to achieve corporate objectives.

► **CHAPTER REVIEW** ◄

1. **Training Strategies**
A training strategy outlines in broad terms the campaign for the training function in any organization. It is a statement of intent and:
- Provides the basis for the implementation of training policies
- Outlines the course of action designed to achieve training objectives

2. To be effective a training strategy must take into consideration many elements which affect the organization and the training function.

3. **SWOT analysis**
A SWOT analysis helps to identify the internal and external factors which influence an organization and, therefore, the training function.

The SWOT matrix evaluates strengths, weaknesses, opportunities and threats.

4. **Training as an agent of change**
The major purpose of training is to achieve improved performance from staff and management. To do so, it effects change in employee knowledge, skills performance or behaviour.

5 The Training Plan

▷   **CHAPTER SUMMARY**   ◁

This chapter analyses the need for the training plan, a practical document used to design and implement training.

- The training plan
- Identification of training needs
- Description of the required training programmes
- The appropriate training methods
- Selection and training of trainers
- Detailed costs and benefits of training

Once your training policies and strategies are defined, you can embark on the development of your training plan. A training plan translates training policy and strategy into tactics – tactics used to design and implement training.

Tactics are the detailed plans or schemes used to implement management policies and strategies.

The Training Plan

The training plan is the launch pad for the design and implementation of your training programmes. A training plan is a practical document which takes into account identified training needs and outlines training programmes to meet those needs.

This, in fact, represents the first two steps of the training function

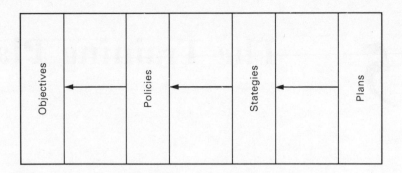

Figure 5.1 *Developing the Training Plan*

listed in Chapter 1 earlier in the book: identifying training needs, and formulating (ie planning and developing) required training.

The training plan identifies training needs and outlines what training programmes and methods will help to meet those needs. See Figure 5.1.

> **Trainer's Tip**
> As a reminder, the last two steps in a systematic approach to training consisted of: the implementation of training, and an assessment of the results of training.

Elements of the training plan

In preparing to write your training plan, it is important to outline your key topics and their sub-headings. The key topics or elements of the training plan are:

- Identification of training needs
- Description of the required training programmes
- The appropriate training methods to be used
- Selection and training of trainers
- Detailed costs and benefits of training

Identification of training needs

It is important to identify all the training needs within an organization as they will vary according to employee, job position, job responsibilities and department. A thorough analysis of training needs is a prerequisite for the design of any training plan, and ensures that each individual employee is sent on the appropriate training courses.

What is a training need?

A training need is usually defined as a gap – the gap between the requirements of a particular job and the capabilities of the employee currently holding the job. However, training needs do not only occur at the level of the job.

Trainer's Tip
Identifying training needs can reveal:
- A knowledge gap
- A skills gap
- An attitude or behaviour problem

- Where past training has failed
- Shortcomings recognized by both manager and employee
- An individual's suitability for promotion

- Where on-job training has meant 'learning from Nellie' (ie learning both suitable and unsatisfactory practices)

There are two basic types of training needs: (1) Organizational, and (2) Individual.

1. *Organizational training needs*

A careful analysis throughout the organization is essential to assess the sum total of training needs. This is to ensure that training will improve performance of the organization as a whole and ensure organizational objectives are met. The gap between achieved results and targeted goals is the training gap.

Determining training needs for the organization involves four basic steps. This process is illustrated in Figure 5.2.

1. To analyse whether organizational targets have been met
2. To determine what knowledge, skills and attitudes are contained within the organization
3. To analyse the actual performance of employees
4. To analyse organizational performance

Organizational needs can also be assessed according to a TOWS analysis, which is a variation of the SWOT analysis. The TOWS analysis is used to examine each of the key activity areas in the

OTN = Organizational Training Needs
KSA = Knowledge, Skills, Attitude

Figure 5.2 *Organizational training needs*

organization: for example, production, distribution, research and development, sales and marketing, finance and accounting, personnel and training.

Activity – TOWS analysis
1. The answers to the following questions can be applied to a TOWS analysis. The TOWS analysis helps to identify organizational needs: we first examine external factors (threats and opportunities), then survey internal factors (weaknesses and strengths).

External factors
- How do customers perceive your products and services?
- What is the reputation and image of the organization?
- What are the key influences on image and reputation?
- What problems does your organization face in the marketplace?
- What influence does training have on these external factors?

- How is the organization perceived in terms of commitment to staff and management training?
- How committed to training are your competitors?
- How does this influence recruitment of new employees?

Internal factors
- How many employees work in the organization?
- Is the organization under-staffed or over-staffed?
- What are the various departments?
- How well does each department function?
- What areas of under-performance have been identified?
- What knowledge or skills are lacking, by department?
- What problems have been experienced in training?
- What are the priorities given to training in each department?
- What is the attitude of senior management and line management to training?
- Are training objectives and programmes linked to achieving corporate objectives?
- What are your key organizational strengths in terms of employee performance?

2. What other questions are relevant to your organization and could be included in this analysis?
3. Once you have completed your TOWS analysis, what changes need to be made to address opportunities and threats?
4. Make a list of the organizational training needs which emerge from this analysis. These points should be addressed in your training plan.

Example
A new four-star hotel recently used the TOWS analysis to assess the needs of all staff. Hotel management wished to determine which staff required training in the first year of opening.

Training needs identified by the TOWS analysis were categorized by departmental products and services. These departments were:

Reception and Sales Administration
- Customer service
- Accommodation – bedrooms and suites

Conference and Banqueting
- Conference and meeting room facilities

        – Conference equipment
        – Catering menus and staff
    Bars and Restaurant
        – Quality of customer service
        – Quality of food and drink
    Leisure Facilities
        – Safety and hygiene factors
        – Customer service

According to this assessment of the hotel and all its employees, training needs were identified as product training, customer care training and sales training.

Product Training: It was agreed that all staff and management would require product training. This was to ensure that every employee understood what facilities were available to guests, to non-residents, and on what days and at what times.

Customer Care Training: The majority of staff and management also needed customer care training. This was to guarantee that a consistently friendly and hospitable image was portrayed at all times. Customer Care training was also seen as an effective way to teach staff how to deal constructively with awkward customers.

Sales Training: It was decided that sales training would be given in the first year of training to conference, banqueting, and the sales and reservations departments. This was because staff and management in these departments would be expected to sell key products: i.e. accommodation, conferences, weddings, dinner dances, and bar and restaurant facilities.

The team running the leisure area were to be given customer care training. At a later date, with the launch and promotion of leisure club membership, sales training would be scheduled.

Individual training needs

Training needs analysis for individuals often begins with an assessment of the job description. Training on an individual basis concerns three key areas:

1. Knowledge
2. Skills
3. Attitude

Figure 5.3 shows the inter-relationship of knowledge, skills and attitudes and their effect on individual performance.

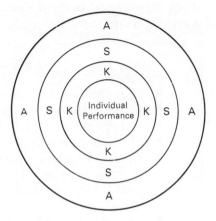

Figure 5.3 *Knowledge, skills and attitude*

Example

An employee working for a local radio station as a publicity officer was promoted to head of the sales and marketing department. In order to adapt to this new position, a training needs analysis was completed to ensure that the employee adjusted quickly and effectively to his new role.

Although this employee had been with the radio station for many years, gaps were identified between his knowledge and skills in the previous position, and those required for the new role.

His attitude was very positive and enthusiastic, but training needs were identified in knowledge and skills required to perform the new job effectively as:

Knowledge:
- Introduction to the basics of marketing theory

Skills:
- Basic management skills to manage a small team
- Sales techniques to handle objections to price
- Time management skills

The checklist below will help you to identify training needs for the organization and the individual. It is divided into general questions about training within the organization, and specific questions about individual performance.

CHECKLIST

1. General
   - What staff training records are available?
   - Have you assessed staff training records?
   - Who maintains employee training records?
   - Are training records regularly updated?
   - When was a skills inventory last done for each area or department? (i.e. clerical, technical, skilled labour, unskilled labour, staff managers, line managers, senior managers, etc)
   - When should you next implement a skills inventory?
   - How can you best balance organizational needs against current employee skill assets?

2. Individual
   - What tasks, knowledge, skills and attitudes must be performed to do each job?
   - What knowledge is required? (eg company or product knowledge)
   - Which skills are lacking? (eg operator, technical, computer, sales, supervisory, management, coaching, training skills)
   - What shortcomings are there in attitude? (eg angers quickly, too timid, too aggressive, speaks before thinking)

Description of the Required Training Programmes

This is the second step in preparing your training plan. Selection and design of training programmes demands much preparation and planning. However, for any training programme it is important to take account of the motivation or drive of the trainees.

Typical motivating factors might be:
- Desire for expertise or success
- Feelings of intimidation or inadequacy
- Fear of failure or rejection
- The need for approval, recognition, or endorsement
- Desire for material gain

- Sheer curiosity or interest in a new challenge
- Standards of training rooms and facilities
- Quality of trainers and training programmes

The checklist, below, in four stages, will help you with the planning and preparation of your training programmes.

CHECKLIST

Stage One

- Draw up a summary of training needs – to establish the main areas and priorities for training.
- Do you have job specifications for each job position?
- Which individuals and which groups need training?
- Have you involved line managers and staff managers at all stages of planning?
- How will participants be consulted and briefed about the training?

Trainer's Tip

A job specification is a detailed statement which specifies the tasks, duties, knowledge, skills, abilities and attitudes required to perform a job satisfactorily.

CHECKLIST

Stage Two

- What training programmes already exist?
- Which new training programmes need to be designed?
- What are the aims, objectives, and programme contents?
- Which training methods are to be employed?
- What are your resources (amount available to spend)?
- What specialized training is required? (eg supervisory, assertiveness, management, etc)

CHECKLIST

Stage Three

- Who are the trainers who will deliver the training?
- What will determine the content of the training programmes?
- Who will be responsible for the design of new courses?
- Where will the training take place?

- Who is responsible for monitoring the results of training?
- How will the training be evaluated and assessed?

Trainer's Tip
According to Buckley and Caple (1990) evaluation is an attempt to measure the overall benefit of training in terms of cost to the organization. We will discuss this in more detail in Chapters 10 and 11.

Assessment (or validation) appraises whether the training objectives have met the needs of the trainees, and whether the trainees have achieved the objectives set by training (ie improved job performance, enhanced knowledge, or improvement in attitude).

CHECKLIST
Stage Four
- Who will co-ordinate the administration for the training courses?
- Who is responsible for the schedule of dates and timing for the training programmes?
- Which programmes will be held on-site and off-site?
- What training equipment is available?
- What additional training equipment needs to be purchased or hired?
- Who is responsible for the training budget?

Trainer's Tip
Administration, timing, training facilities and equipment all rely on the overall training budget. Who will be responsible for monitoring this budget?

The Appropriate Training Methods

A training plan describes the training methods to be used in delivering training within the organization. The number of training methods available are many and varied, and certain methods may be better suited to your training programmes. The most appropriate form of training depends on the following variables:

- Your set training objectives
- The skills, experience and expertise of your trainers
- Available training facilities and materials
- The learning abilities of your trainees

Trainers should work with the training methods which are best suited to them individually. An alternative is to use team-teaching, or to recruit an external training consultant if a trainer is particularly uncomfortable with a particular teaching method (eg role-playing).

However, a variety of methods will ensure successful and interesting training programmes, and is more likely to satisfy the needs of the organization and the individual. Below is a fairly comprehensive list of what is available to you and your team as trainers.

Training methods

1. A lecture
A talk given by an expert who asks for audience questions and participation at the end.

2. A demonstration
Showing a group how best to handle a situation or set of procedures. Time should be allowed for trainees to practise the new skills or techniques.

3. A participative lesson
A lesson which encourages interaction between trainer and trainees. It can take the route of question and answer, exercises and case studies.

4. Individual coaching
Tutorial coaching is usually done on a one-to-one basis. The advantage of this method is that individual counselling and appraisal can be used in conjunction with set tasks and targets.

5. A tutor-led group discussion
An activity led by a trainer who guides the group discussion to achieve certain training objectives. It encourages a high level of participation from trainees, and allows opportunity for opinions to be shared and expressed.

6. Role-playing
In role-playing, trainees are presented with a situation which is as near to the real working environment as possible. The problem is to be resolved by acting out roles and resolving a particular situation.

Role-playing may involve using the telephone, in-tray exercises, selling situations, handling customer complaints, case studies, business games, etc.

7. Critical incident

This is a group training method where participants describe incidents in a given period which have presented them with problems. The basic facts of each situation are discussed and the trainees decide what further information and training is required to solve the problem.

8. Training games

A game or exercise in which members of a group take part to show how jobs and functions are interrelated. In many games there is an element of competition, and the delegates may be given roles to adopt for the duration of the game.

9. Distance learning

This enables trainees to learn in their own time and at their own pace from training material which is prepared in advance. It can include an interactive-video programme, computer-based training, or a self-teach training manual.

10. Computer-based training (CBT)

CBT is basically a type of training programme delivered by the use of a computer. CBT is inter-active and caters to a trainee's needs on an individual basis. CBT simulates actual situations and encourages the trainee to learn by doing.

11. Interactive video

This combines computer-based training and video. Use of the computer allows for individual pacing, and the video offers a more realistic picture of working situations.

12. Self-teach training manual

This is a self-training workbook which is edited and laid out for simple use. The manual can be used to reinforce knowledge and understanding of training points or subjects.

13. Case study

The case study provides for the study, analysis and discussion of a real situation. Often used in training courses for managers and supervisors to achieve competence and understanding.

14. On-job instruction

Used primarily for training in manual tasks. The tutor's presentation usually consists of show and tell, or explanation and demonstration.

15. Packaged programmes

These are often off-the-shelf packages with set timetables, lessons, exercises and case studies. They can include training manuals, audio visual aids, and instructions for the tutor.

16. Programmed instruction

This training method can be used by individuals or groups. It organizes material in a logical, step-by-step programme. Programmed instruction is training in stages, and may take the form of a training manual, visual aids, or be part of a computer or interactive video programme.

17. An assignment, task or project

This may be a specific task or project set by a trainee's manager to enhance skills or knowledge by resolving an actual problem within the organization.

Selection and Training of Trainers

This subject will be covered in greater detail in Part II, 'Managing the Training Team'. A few key points are relevant at this stage.

Training plans describe the tactics and methods to be used by your trainers, but the selection of methods depends on trainer ability and expertise.

Your training plan should describe each trainer's ability to select, design and deliver training programmes to meet organizational needs. This will be affected by the following key factors:

- The type of training methods to be used
- Current expertise and skills of your trainers
- Your trainers' training needs
- The constraints of the training facilities
- The investment of time and money in your trainers

What is most important is to constantly evaluate the effectiveness of your training team, and analyse feedback gained from both trainers and trainees in post-training debriefings.

Detailed Costs and Benefits of Training

We will develop this subject in Part III, 'Your Training Budget – The Financial Return'. But, a few words on the subject are important now because your training plan should include a final section on:

- The financial costs of your training programme
- The available finances and structure of the training budget
- The benefits of training to the organization and its employees

Costs

Armstrong (1988) noted that the basic costs for training are: remuneration and expenses of trainers and trainees; preparation and maintenance of training programmes; training materials, equipment and premises; lower performance of trainees until fully trained.

These costs can be broken down into seven specific cost areas to be considered in your training plan:

1. Salaries, wages and expenses of trainers
2. Trainee expenses (eg travel costs, meals and accommodation)
3. Costs to prepare training programmes
4. Support and upkeep of training programmes
5. Cost of training materials, equipment and premises
6. Training of trainers to improve their knowledge, skills and job performance
7. Financial losses to the company due to continuing inadequate employee performance.

Benefits

The benefits of training can be plotted in terms of benefits for employees and benefits for the organization.

Individual benefits:
- More job satisfaction
- Improved job performance
- Better career prospects
- Greater salary expectations

Organizational benefits:
- Improves work performance
- Increases safety at work
- Reinforces staff motivation
- More consistent customer satisfaction

Conclusion

In this chapter we identified the training plan as a practical document which details the tactics used to design and implement training.

The training plan outlines what training programmes and methods can be used to meet organizational and individual training needs.

► **CHAPTER REVIEW** ◄

1. The training plan
A training plan translates training policy and strategy into tactics. The elements of this practical document are:

- Identification of training needs
- Description of the required training programmes
- The appropriate training methods
- Selection and training of trainers
- Detailed costs and benefits of training

2. Identification of training needs
A training need is the gap between the requirements of a particular job and the capabilities of the employee currently holding the job.
There are two basic types of training needs: organizational and individual.

3. The appropriate training methods
A training plan briefly describes the training methods to be used in delivery of training programmes. Various methods include:

- A lecture
- A demonstration
- A participative lesson
- Individual coaching
- A tutor-led group discussion
- Role-playing
- Critical incident
- Training games
- Distance learning
- Computer-based training (CBT)
- Interactive video
- Self-teach training manual
- Case study
- On-job instruction
- Packaged programmes
- Programmed instruction
- Assignment, task or project

4. Selection and training of trainers
Training plans describe the tactics and methods to be used by your trainers. Key factors to influence the selection and evaluation of your training team are:

- Type of training methods to be used
- Current expertise and skills of your trainers
- Your trainers' training needs
- The constraints of the training facilities
- The investment of time and money in your trainers

5. Detailed costs and benefits of training
Training plans should evaluate the costs and benefits of the training function.

6 The Training Team and their Skills

▷   CHAPTER SUMMARY   ◁

In this chapter we will examine the many roles of the trainer, and what should be expected of your training team.

- The practical role of the trainer
- Taking stock of your trainers
- Trainer competence levels
- Analysis of trainer skills

The development of the training plan requires a thorough review of the skills and performance of your trainers. It is critical that your team can cope effectively with the demands of training within the organization.

The Practical Role of the Trainer

The main roles of a trainer are those of:

- Facilitator (enabling participants to learn)
- Deliverer (presenter of training)

A trainer may be expected to fulfil other roles to maintain credibility and to deliver successful training programmes. For instance the trainer may be a:

- subject expert
- technical adept
- authority on methodology
- manager of people
- coach and counsellor
- consultant and adviser

- facilitator and assistant
- organiser and motivator
- leader and role model
- planner and organizer
- creator and designer
- administrator and supervisor

Taking Stock of your Trainers

To ascertain what skills are needed to deliver training effectively within the organization, it is vital to take stock of your trainers. A first step is to take an inventory of the training team. In Chapter 19 we examine the theoretical role of the trainer.

- What is the image of the trainer in your organization?
- How many trainers are in your team?
- Are you a self-contained department?
- What is your department's relationship to line management?
- How long have your trainers worked as trainers?
- What is the background and experience of your training team?
- What are the career patterns of your trainers?
- What opportunities are there to develop your team?

What is the image of the trainer in your organization?

Before launching an analysis of the knowledge, skills and behaviour of your current training team, consider how the trainer is perceived by the organization and its employees.

Are your trainers seen to be instructors, lecturers, performers or tutors? Or all of these? Are they rated equally in terms of professionalism, ability and performance? If not, why not?

> **Activity**
> 1. Make a list of all the positive and negative factors which contribute to the image and reputation of your training team.
> 2. Based on this list and the size of your training team, what steps can you take to increase the credibility of your trainers?
> 3. What do your trainers feel about this?

How many trainers are in your team?

The success of the training function will depend on available resources, and your trainers are your greatest resource. It does not matter if there is one trainer or ten. What is significant is that the number of training programmes you propose to implement takes into account the number of trainers available.

The credibility of your trainers is an important factor in any organization, particularly if you are pioneering the path for training. Credibility rests on your team's ability to:

- Implement training programmes effectively
- Maintain scheduled dates and times of courses
- Provide the right type and number of courses
- Maintain an image of professional and competent trainers

Are you a self-contained department?

Some training departments represent one section of the personnel function, and therefore share administrative and managerial facilities. If, as head of training, you are part of another department, it is important to supervise the amount of time devoted to training.

An effective training department is a cohesive department where trainers work well together and motivate each other. The training team will be more successful if all trainers share the various training tasks:

- analysing training needs
- administrating (unless a training administrator manages this role)
- selecting, designing and delivering the training programmes

What is your department's relationship to line management?

The responsibility of line managers must not be neglected when taking stock of the role of your trainers. Line managers fulfil a useful function as coaches, counsellors and advisers.

Being concerned with managing, briefing, counselling, advising and motivating staff, line management responsibilities go hand in hand with the functions of training. One obvious way to involve line management is to conduct a survey; this will determine what line managers perceive as training priorities in their own departments.

Although this type of survey may result in subjective responses, it fulfils two purposes. First, managers and supervisors will be committed to training from the beginning, and this will encourage their support. Second, it gives the training department a starting point from which to analyse training needs.

How long have your trainers worked as trainers?

The length of time your trainers have worked as 'trainers' can influence the perception of training within the organization.

In many firms, managers and supervisors are moved from another department into training (or into personnel and training) because: either a training vacancy exists; they are ready for promotion and no other position is available; or they are near to retirement.

None the less, trainer motivation and commitment is essential to build an active and inspired team of trainers. Your present training arrangements may be deficient if your trainers do not perceive themselves to be 'trainers', but rather managers seconded for a period of time from another division.

What is the background and experience of your training team?

Trainer motivation is relevant to both the working environment, and to the background and experience of your trainers. If they have not trained as trainers, feelings of inadequacy may exist. This can lead to lack of confidence, inferior delivery of programmes and possible demotivation of trainees.

A broad job analysis can highlight the demands of the job, and indicate the strengths and weaknesses of your trainers. It will help you to determine:

- How your trainers see the purpose of their job
- Current trainer knowledge, skills and attitudes
- Primary knowledge and skills required
- Strengths and weaknesses in performance
- What action is required

What are the career patterns of your trainers?

An analysis of each trainer's curriculum vitae prior to holding an informal discussion with them to discuss the pattern of their careers, will help you to:

- Discern trainers' attitudes to the job
- Ascertain their suitability to the role of trainer

This evaluation of individual trainers will provide a broader understanding of why each trainer has been selected, and what their true feelings are about their position. This helps you to determine if any trainers feel that their real position is elsewhere in the organization, and can help you decide how to motivate them.

> **Trainer's Tip – Motivation**
> There are many theories on motivation. The best-known theorists are Maslow, Herzberg, McGregor and Vroom.
> The *International Dictionary of Management* (Johannsen & Page 1990) cites three main stages in the process of motivation:
>
> 1. Identify an unsatisfied need
> 2. Define the objective to satisfy the need
> 3. Take action to achieve the objective

What opportunities are there to develop your team?

A thorough analysis of your training team would include an analysis of each trainer's job description and job specification, supplemented by a personal discussion with each trainer. This puts you in a position to:

- determine the current status of the training team
- draw up a training needs analysis
- decide whether new trainers are required to complement your existing team

> **Trainer's Tip**
> A *job description* contains the following elements:
> - The job title
> - Where the job is positioned within the organization
> - The main purpose of the job
> - The primary activities to be carried out
> - The expected standards of performance for the job
> - What contact is to be maintained with other colleagues and departments
> - A definition of the job holder's authority and responsibilities
>
> A *job specification*, on the other hand, breaks down the tasks to be carried out in a particular job. The characteristics of the job holder are highlighted according to what knowledge, skills and attitudes are required.

Trainer Competence Levels

Trainers are required to be competent and proficient in a number of different areas. An analysis of trainer competencies will define what knowledge, skills and attitudes are required by your trainers, and what are their training needs.

Knowledge competence

The trainer's role demands competence in many areas of learning. For example, product knowledge, technical proficiency and computer know-how will all depend on the demands of your organization.

The following topics are suggested areas of competence for trainer knowledge. What else would your team add to the list?

- Motivations for learning
- How learning can be effective
- Barriers to learning
- Training methods
- Product and technical expertise
- Use of training aids
- Design of training courses
- Methods to evaluate and validate training

Trainer's Tip

For learning to be effective the training room should present a favourable environment to learning. In addition to a conducive learning environment, trainers need to:

- motivate trainees
- set standards of performance
- act as mentor and counsellor
- guarantee satisfaction
- encourage active participation

- vary training methods
- be flexible
- observe that trainees operate at different speeds
- allow time to assimilate learning

Motivation plays an essential part in training; it is the reason why employees perform and behave in the way they do. Based on two simple precepts – those of satisfying needs and achieving goals – employees can be motivated by a need to know or by the determination to attain a goal.

Skills competence

The following list suggests general skills competence levels. As this list is not definitive, what other items can you and your team add to the list?

- Analysis of jobs and tasks
- Evaluation of training needs
- Preparation and design of courses
- Design and use of visual aids
- Presenter and manager of training programmes
- Facilitator of learning
- Production of course handouts

Attitude competence

Part of a trainer's role is to observe and evaluate the behaviour of trainees. Trainees are as strongly influenced by the attitudes of the trainer as by work environment and corporate culture.

Trainer perception of the training role is biased due to the organization's support (or lack of support) for the training function, and the trainer's personal attitude to training.

Organizational features

- The culture of the organization
- The style of management
- Leadership effectiveness
- Attitudes of management and colleagues to training
- Support given to training

Personal attitudes

- Personal aims and goals
- Individual motivation factors
- Personal commitment to the job and to the organization
- Ability to change and adapt to situations and people
- Background and experience
- Individual trainer personality

> **Activity**
> The components of a knowledge, skills and attitude analysis include:
>
> - Breaking the job of trainer into its component parts
> - Analysing which tasks are required to be performed
> - Determining what knowledge, skills and behaviour are needed to be competent
>
> Spend an hour making a list of the knowledge, skills and behaviour required by your trainers to fulfil their role to a level of competence. You may wish to do this in a brainstorming session with all the trainers on your team.
>
> If you are the only one in the training department, or a member of a very small team, it is just as important to complete this exercise to determine the gaps and training needs for yourself or your team of trainers.

Analysis of Trainer Skills

Trainers require a number of skills. Not least among them is the ability to structure a training session. Bearing in mind the number of roles a trainer needs to fulfil within the course of a career, basic trainer skills are:

- analytical skills
- technical skills
- computer skills
- interpersonal skills
- counselling skills
- writing skills
- managerial skills
- time management skills
- presentation skills

Having conducted an analysis of required trainer competence levels, the next step is to analyse the current skills of your training team. Although a skills analysis is a prerequisite for all staff, it is especially important to undertake a systematic analysis of the skills of your trainers.

An analysis of the skills of your training team

A first step would be to conduct an inventory of the collective experience, background and status of your trainers within the organization.

What skills do your trainers need?

The second step is to analyse the skills your trainers need to implement the necessary training within the organization. An analysis of their activities helps to determine which skills are needed. These activities include the ability to:

- undertake individual coaching
- run group training sessions
- advise and counsel
- manage distance learning
- design, write and produce a wide range of training materials
- administrate training
- clarify and solve problems

The checklist will help to clarify the skills which your trainers presently bring to the training department, and which skills your team needs to develop.

CHECKLIST

1. Which skills do your trainers possess?
2. What additional skills are essential to carry out training properly?
3. Which training methods are your training team accustomed to using? (**For example:** assignments, exercises, games, case studies, coaching, group discussion, job instruction, lectures, computer-based training, packaged programmes, role-playing, interactive learning.)
4. Are your trainers simply facilitators, or are they flexible in their use of training methods? (**For example:** The trainer as facilitator enables trainees to learn by themselves. The flexible trainer chooses the best method for the learning situation and for the development of the particular individual or group. A suitable exercise might be: a tutor running a session on presentation skills asks each trainee to present a five-minute talk. The group is divided into four working pairs. Each pair guides and counsels their partner in preparation for the presentation; they are given ten guidelines. After the presentation, all the participants offer constructive comments with a closing review by the tutor.)
5. Can your trainers design, write and deliver their own programmes? (If not, who is responsible for this role? It is essential that time be allotted to this aspect of training.)

---

6. What are your trainers' current commitments? (administrative, productive, direct training.)
7. How much time is given to each aspect of the training function?
8. Where is improvement needed?
9. What courses are included in your syllabus?
10. What courses can each trainer provide?
11. What is your role in relation to the tutors, and what help should you offer them?
12. What coaching, counselling and training is offered to your trainers?
13. Are they trained on a regular basis?
14. Are they trained to deliver new subjects?
15. What are their training needs? (**For example:** product knowledge, new skills, technical or computer techniques.)
16. Which new courses or training programmes are needed? (This will be related to the analysis of organizational and individual training needs.)

Conclusion

This chapter looked at the many roles of the trainer. It is essential to ascertain what knowledge and skills are needed to deliver training within the organization, and to evaluate the levels of competence within your training team. Whatever the role of the trainer, flexibility is essential at all times.

> ► **CHAPTER REVIEW** ◄

1. The role of the trainer
Many and varied roles are expected of a trainer. The two key roles are those of:
    - facilitator (enabling participants to learn)
    - deliverer (presenter of training)
2. Taking stock of your trainers
A first step is to take an inventory of your training team. Eight questions will help determine the credibility of your team:
    - What is the image of the trainer in your organization?
    - How many trainers are in your team?
    - Are you a self-contained department?
    - What is your department's relationship to line management?
    - How long have your trainers worked as trainers?
    - What is the background and experience of your training team?
    - What are the career patterns of your trainers?
    - What opportunities are there to develop your team?
3. Credibility rests on your team's ability to:
    - Implement training programmes effectively
    - Maintain scheduled dates and times of courses
    - Provide the right type and number of courses
    - Maintain an image of professional and competent trainers
4. Trainer competence levels
    - Knowledge competence
    - Skills competence
    - Attitude competence

7 The Trainer as Consultant

▷   **CHAPTER SUMMARY**   ◁

This chapter looks in detail at the internal trainer as consultant. We refer to this role as the trainer consultant.

- What is a trainer consultant?
- The importance of feedback
- Consultancy skills

In addition to the roles of facilitator and deliverer, the trainer must be a planner, administrator and in-house consultant. An illustration of how these roles interrelate is shown in Figure 7.1.

What is a Trainer Consultant?

A trainer working on special projects or as a problem solver within the organization is a trainer consultant. These activities usually have a link to training.

To perform the role of consultant competently, a trainer requires expertise as an adviser, motivator, and diagnostician – with a high degree of interpersonal skills. This is because, as an internal consultant, the trainer:

- Promotes understanding within the organization
- Ascertains what problems or needs exist
- Identifies those needs in relation to individuals or the organization

67

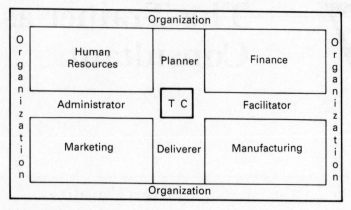

T C = Training Consultant

Figure 7.1 *The Trainer as consultant*

- Helps discern what is preventing the achievement of organizational targets
- Acts as a problem solver

Expertise in analytical skills and learning methods helps the trainer to identify problems and propose a way forward to solve them.

These trainer skills play a major part in adopting what is essentially a catalyst role. The trainer (and specifically the training manager) objectively assesses each department and assimilates information to try and understand departmental views, opinions and needs.

Problems may relate to:

- Organizational targets to be achieved
- Employee needs to perform competently
- Training needs, such as lack of skills – eg sales skills, business correspondence skills, copywriting skills, supervisory or management skills

- Attitude and behaviour problems specific to an individual or department – eg arrogance, temper, bad manners, personal hygiene factors
- Inadequate knowledge – eg company, product, technical, plant or engineering knowledge
- Lack of resources – funds, facilities, manpower
- Restricted time prior to a product launch, promotion, exhibition, trade show, etc.

> **Trainer's Tip**
> Learning and work should be integrated if employees are to be given the chance to learn from the challenges and problems which arise in the working environment.
> Whatever problem the 'trainer consultant' is asked to help solve, particular attention should be paid to organizational and individual training needs, the process of motivation, individual participation in the training process, providing satisfaction from learning, and maintaining support as a follow-up to training.

Tasks of the trainer consultant

The training manager is well placed within the organization to act as a consultant. Due to specific observation and diagnostic skills, interpersonal skills, and knowledge of the organization and its employees, the tasks which the trainer consultant may be asked to handle are to:

- Provide expertise and reduce managerial workload
- Identify a problem
- Evaluate a problem (to determine symptoms and root causes)

- Select personnel to be involved in problem-solving
- Analyse and evaluate information and data
- Discuss how to resolve a problem
- Plan the action to settle the problem

- Estimate the costs to solve the problem
- Write the report of overall findings and the action to be taken
- Follow-up and evaluate
- Brief management on results and findings

Example – Special Project

Decline in sales

In a pharmaceutical organization, the sales director noticed that sales of a new product range were declining in the first quarter of the financial year. This was despite the success of existing products in the company's portfolio.

Brainstorming

The sales team was called in by the sales director to brainstorm on the possible reasons for this lack of success. The training manager was also invited to join the group. The entire team had recently undergone a training programme in face-to-face sales skills; the objective of the programme had been to introduce sales skills to the team to improve their performance in obtaining sales for all products.

At the meeting, market figures were discussed and the recent sales figures were analysed. Although competitive firms were doing well, it was a high growth market and there should have been no reason for the new high quality range not to sell.

The trainer consultant

The training manager suggested that a trainer be assigned to travel with each of the field sales representatives; this was impractical. A sample of four from the eight representatives were selected, and the trainer spent a day with each one.

The objective of the exercise was to determine if the recently implemented training had had the desired effect, or if further training was required.

After four days of travelling with half the sales team, the trainer reported back to the sales director and the training manager. The trainer had seen at first hand that, despite sales training, the field sales team were not yet confident in closing the sale on the new product range. As a result, they rarely asked for the order! The existing products within the range were so well established that they virtually sold themselves.

Sales training proposed

A two-day training session was designed and planned to concentrate on closing techniques. The training methods used were group discussion and role-playing.

The role-playing sessions were followed up by a second trip into the field by the trainer with the other four sales representatives. This was to ascertain whether closing techniques had been successfully adopted by the field sales team.

Resolving the problem

The sales representatives had gained a good deal of confidence following the practical role-playing sessions, and began to close the sale more effectively and more often.

Unit sales began to increase and the training manager, acting as consultant, suggested that a more structured and systematic approach to training be adopted within the sales department.

The Importance of Feedback

The above case study illustrates the importance of feedback in all training situations, and shows how the trainer consultant can help resolve organizational problems and assist in the achievement of key targets.

Feedback or communication is needed (and can fail) at three levels in training. This is between:

1. Trainees and line managers (pre- and post-training)
2. Trainees and trainers (during a training session)
3. Trainers and line managers (pre- and post-training)

There should be feedback, whether positive or negative, from trainees participating in a training session. The tutor requires this feedback both during and after a course to determine:

- If the trainee understood the subject material
- What retention level has been achieved
- What action is to be taken at the end of the course
- Whether that action has been successfully executed

Feedback ensures that the training has been valuable; encourages interaction between the key players in training (trainees, line managers and trainers); and guarantees that the trainer is well-placed to fulfil the role of consultant when needed (ie adviser and problem-solver).

A checklist will help you to determine what procedures should be set up to obtain sufficient feedback to analyse the results of training.

CHECKLIST
1. What formal procedures are set up for trainees to give feedback to the trainer at the end of training?
2. What feedback do trainers give to the head of training at the end of a training programme? (eg at a weekly, monthly meeting.)
3. Is that information analysed and evaluated?
4. What formal procedures are in place for trainers to brief the head of training following direct training?
5. What follow-up procedures are in place to determine if the training objectives have been achieved? (eg the trainee learnt sufficient about a new software package to begin to apply it competently on the job.)
6. Do these procedures include a trainee debriefing session with an immediate supervisor or line manager?
7. What contact do trainers have with line management at the end of a training programme?

Consultancy Skills

Trainer consultants should be flexible enough to take sufficient account of three factors: the problem, the personnel involved, and organizational pressures. It is important to consider whether the existing personnel can set in motion the proposed action plans. If this is impossible, then it may be necessary to revise your action to suit your circumstances.

If you delegate the role of trainer consultant to one of your trainers:

- Brief the trainer consultant carefully and clearly.
- Give every assistance to the trainer consultant in defining the problem and the specific task requirements.
- Clarify how the role of consultant will affect direct training responsibilities, and which projects take priority.
- Ensure that arrangements are made to meet regularly with other managers who are involved in a particular project.
- Periodically assess the direction and scope of the project.

Communication, interviewing and counselling

In assessing the skills of your trainers and whether they are qualified to act as internal consultants, the following questions will assist you:

1. Are your trainers capable of interviewing and counselling? This is when the trainer's interpersonal and communication skills are most needed – eg asking the right type of questions and listening.
2. What training is required to top-up interviewing and counselling skills? All trainers should be well trained in the art of interviewing and counselling.
3. What follow-up takes place after each training session? Are procedures in place to ensure follow-up happens as a matter of course?
4. As head of training, do you debrief your managers? What happens during your debriefing session? What should happen? Do you follow-up this debriefing session?
5. What procedures are set up to communicate with line management at the end of each training session? How difficult is it to implement these? What can you do to improve the situation?
6. Do your debriefing and feedback procedures allow flexibility? (eg to advise and brief management as to what further training, if any, is required.)

Trainer's Tip

The consultancy process can be made more effective if all trainers and managers are well trained in interviewing and counselling techniques.

Points for the trainer consultant to consider prior to any problem-solving interview are:

- To create a comfortable environment which will encourage the interviewee to participate
- To approach the interview and the interviewee with an open mind and a positive attitude
- To be prepared to listen 60 per cent of the time and speak 40 per cent of the time
- To respect the confidentiality of the interviewee
- To have a list of topics to cover to begin the interview
- To be flexible
- To refrain from being judgemental

Conclusion

In this chapter we have examined the role of the trainer as an internal consultant within the organization. The trainer consultant's expertise in the areas of analysis, motivation and learning are invaluable in identifying, evaluating and helping to resolve individual and organizational problems.

Trainer consultants should take account of the problems, the resources and organizational pressures relevant to the issue at hand. This may involve evaluation of feedback as a result of direct training sessions, or consultation for special projects which relate to training.

Although the trainer should be well skilled in eliciting feedback from all personnel (trainees, staff and managers), skill in communicating, interviewing and counselling is essential for the trainer consultant.

▶   **CHAPTER REVIEW**   ◀

1. **The trainer consultant**
   The trainer acts as an internal consultant within the organization on special projects or as a problem solver. These projects usually have a link to training.

2. **An internal consultant**
   The trainer is an internal consultant and works within the organization to:

   - Promote understanding
   - Identify problems
   - Examine why targets are not achieved
   - Act as a problem solver

3. **The importance of feedback**
   Effective communication and feedback during and after direct training can succeed or fail at three levels of communication – ie between:

   1. Trainees and line managers
   2. Trainees and trainers
   3. Trainers and line managers

4. A checklist will help to determine what procedures should be set up to promote positive feedback during and after training.
   Feedback:

   - Ensures training has been valuable
   - Encourages interaction between trainees, trainers and line managers
   - Guarantees the trainer is well-placed to fulfil the role of internal consultant

5. **Consultancy skills**
   Trainer consultants need to take account of the issues, the personnel and the pressures within the organization when tackling any problem.
   Selected skills are required for any trainer in a consultancy role (eg interviewing and counselling skills).

8 Training Administration

▷   CHAPTER SUMMARY   ◁

This chapter examines the critical role of the training administrator. The training administrator plays an important role in:

- Managing training administration
- The production of training notes
- Selection of training facilities

Effective administration of the training function can ensure the success of training within the organization.

The training administrator relieves the trainer of organizational problems prior to delivery of the training session, and provides administrative support to the trainer whose time should be fully devoted to the training itself.

Managing Training Administration

Although the quality of the trainer is of paramount importance in the successful delivery of any training programme, the administration that takes place behind the scenes is of equal value.

Effective administration of programme times and schedules, booking venues, producing course materials, and the purchase or hire of training equipment are details that ensure the success of every training course. Tasks to be considered are:

- Joining instructions (course and venue information)

- Accommodation reservations
- Menu planning
- Coffee and tea breaks

- Recreational facilities
- Production of course handouts

- Booking of visual aids
- Layout of the training room
- Trainee materials
- Trainer materials
- Liaison with line managers
- Pre- and post-course briefing of trainees

Joining instructions

Joining instructions for trainees should be sent well in advance of the course. Information provided should include:

Course information:
- Aims and objectives of the training course
- Programme contents
- Timings of the programme
- Names of the trainers
- Materials to be supplied

Venue information:
- Name and location of the training venue
- Accommodation and services to be provided
- Expected trainee expenditure
- Car parking facilities
- Required dress

Accommodation reservations

Advance confirmation of costs, reservations and dates should be made to trainees. Directions and a suitable map should be included to ensure trainees arrive on time at the selected destination. Accommodation should be booked as necessary for trainees, trainers and guests sitting in on the course.

Menu planning/coffee breaks

Requests for special meals can be solicited prior to the training programme, and mention made of times for coffee, tea and smoking breaks. This is when time can be allotted for messages and calls back to the office; indication should be made of telephone and fax numbers to be left with office colleagues.

Recreational facilities

During a longer course, it is useful for trainees to relax and enjoy recreational facilities that may be nearby or part of the training venue. However, there is nothing more frustrating to delegates than to arrive at a venue and then discover gym or pool facilities. Preparing delegates in advance means they can choose whether or not to use available facilities.

Production of course handouts

It is essential that any course handouts are professionally presented, and if possible a file or folder should be provided within which they can be kept. If possible, the corporate logo should be on all training materials.

The trainer should always mention what handouts are to be passed out during a course, and inform delegates from the beginning what notes they can be expected to take during the training session.

Booking of visual aids

An administrator responsible for booking visual aids would be well advised to keep a list of equipment which each venue has available; which equipment trainers themselves provide; and what equipment requires booking for each course. The type of equipment needed may be: slide projector, overhead projector, spare bulbs, screen, white boards, free-standing flip charts, blank flip chart pads and marker pens.

Layout of the training room

The physical learning environment is one of the first impressions a delegate has of a training course. The room layout can be highly influential in the success of the training course. It can ensure:

- Effective communication between trainer and trainees
- Maximum comfort of trainees
- Adequate visibility of both trainer and visual aids

Suitable layout of the training furniture (dependent on room size and the number of delegates) helps to achieve course objectives; proper lighting prevents delegate eye strain; and windows or air conditioning ensure comfortable room temperature.

> **Trainer's Tip**
> Room layout can take many shapes and is essential for adequate note taking, viewing of visual aids, and management of delegate participation. Various methods may include:
> - Boardroom style with delegates and tutor around a main table
> - Classroom style to accommodate large numbers
> - Conference layout which gives individual groups their own table for concentrated group work
> - Group circle for small, informal discussions
> - Horseshoe or U-shape for small numbers
> - Theatre-style for large or formal lectures
>
> See Figure 8.1 for graphic illustrations of room layout.

Trainee materials

These are the materials the trainee may require during the training session. They include:

- blank paper, files, pens and pencils, pencil sharpener, rulers, hole punch, stapler, scissors, marking pens, calculators, computers, VDU screens, reference books, training manuals and training films

Trainer materials

There is nothing more frustrating than for a trainer to be in the middle of a session and have the light go out on the overhead projector with no spare bulb to hand, or to be in the middle of a closed circuit TV session and to run out of video tapes. Other required materials may be:

- paper clips, marker pens, temporary adhesive pads, hole punch, scissors, spare flip chart pads, extension cables, sticky tape, rubber bands, clear acetates, blank index file cards, name plates or labels, video cartridges, course handouts and course certificates.
- computers, tables and chairs for computer-based training (CBT), TV monitor, microphone and video for closed-circuit television (CCTV), keys to lock the training room for security purposes.

79

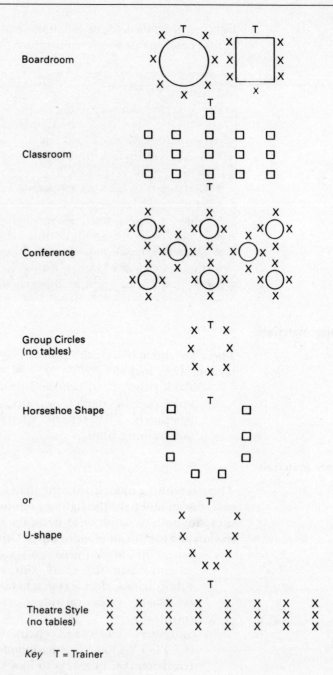

Boardroom

Classroom

Conference

Group Circles
(no tables)

Horseshoe Shape

or

U-shape

Theatre Style
(no tables)

Key T = Trainer

Figure 8.1 *Alternative room layouts*

- in-house training packages (these may include off-the-shelf packages, distance learning packages, computer-based training packages).

Liaison with line managers

Prior to any course, line management should brief the trainee about the benefits of attending the selected course. This should be in addition to the meetings between trainer and line manager to ensure both parties are clear about training objectives, content of the course, anticipated action plans, and course follow-up.

Pre- and post-course briefing of trainees

Many delegates find they are asked to attend a course at very short notice, or are instructed to attend a course with no briefing at all. This can lead to resentment, lack of motivation, or even feelings of inadequacy by the trainee.

Therefore, a clear trainee briefing prior to the course is essential, followed by an end-of-course debriefing between manager and trainee. This helps to ensure that course training objectives are met.

The Production of Training Notes

Who is responsible for writing training material in your training department? Whether it be an individual trainer, or a team of trainers and administrators, the primary objective is to provide clear, explicit notes which complement the training activities.

It is prudent for all trainers to be skilled in the art of writing training notes; this is an activity which requires time for brainstorming, planning, research, writing and evaluation. Training materials may include:

- Course handouts
- Course exercises (games, case studies, etc)
- Prepared overhead acetates
- 35mm slides
- Illustrations, graphs, maps
- Video packages
- Training films

> **Trainer's Tip – Brainstorming**
>
> Sometimes called buzz groups, brainstorming is a useful way to generate new ideas or approaches to a problem. A practical exercise involving two or more people, brainstorming can produce a greater number of ideas than can be generated by an individual alone.
>
> The idea of the brainstorming session is that each group member suggests ideas or solutions without inhibition. No suggestion is rejected at this stage. The main purpose is to provoke the subconscious to produce an idea that will solve the problem.
>
> All ideas generated by the session should be noted, however impractical. A master list of ideas is then evaluated point by point to determine which items have potential.

Structure of training notes

Training notes and the accompanying practical exercises form an integral part of any training session; they will enhance learning, interest the delegates and motivate them into action. Training notes should follow a logical, chronological sequence complementary to the structure of the training course.

Training notes provide an effective learning tool during the course, and act as a reference guide after completion of the course. During the training programme, notes can be used to promote discussion and debate and to stress key points.

The golden rules when designing training notes are:

- Introduce the subject
- Explain the subject
- Summarize the subject
- Each new subject should ideally emphasize three key points

- Avoid jargon
- Use short, simple sentences
- Write clearly and plainly
- Use positives, avoid negatives
- Write informally using the second person

> **Trainer's Tip: An Outline for Course Handouts**
> 1. The introductory pages describe:
>   - Course objectives
>   - Course content

- Course timings
- Names of delegates participating
2. The body of the notes provides:
   - In-depth information on key training topics
   - Illustrations, graphs, matrixes for emphasis
   - A glossary of relevant new terms
   - Duplicates of trainer acetates or slides
3. Training exercises should:
   - Follow each section of information
   - Help delegates to practise skills or knowledge
   - Allow time for individual pace of learning and/or group discussion and planning

Selection of Training Facilities

One of the primary activities in planning training is to select suitable training venues. Some organizations have in-house training rooms, others book space outside the organization. What training facilities are available for your training sessions?

Visiting, assessing, selecting and booking a training venue is a time-consuming activity. Not only does it require an expert eye to assess the size of the room, suitability of the room and facilities. It also requires the ability to negotiate a price. Some of the factors to be considered are:

- Size of the training rooms
- Suitable syndicate rooms
- Lighting, heating, air conditioning
- Electrical power points
- Available equipment
- Furniture: tables, chairs
- Mobile fixtures: eg white boards, tables, TV stands
- Audio visual equipment
- Catering facilities
- Recreational facilities
- Accommodation facilities
- Access to business facilities (telephone, fax, photocopy)
- Availability of conference staff at the venue

The checklist will assist the training administrator in planning and organizing the facilities needed for training:

CHECKLIST

Internal Facilities

1. Who is responsible for organizing and booking in-house training facilities?
2. What in-house facilities are available for your training sessions?
3. What space is available to be used for direct training and for syndicate rooms?
4. What equipment is available for training on a full-time and part-time basis?
5. Which pieces of equipment need replacing and when?
6. What equipment are trainers responsible for?
7. What new equipment need you purchase over the next three years?
8. What will be the annual cost of replacing worn equipment?

External Facilities

1. What external facilities (venues and equipment) do you require?
2. Who selects and books these external facilities?
3. Who is the contact person at each venue?
4. What are the sizes of the training rooms?
5. What syndicate rooms can be used?
6. What equipment is available and at what cost?
7. How does the hire of facilities fit into your budget?
8. What accommodation and recreational facilities exist at each venue?
9. What business facilities can be used by both trainers and delegates?

Conclusion

The role of the training administrator in assisting the training function cannot be underestimated.

Effective administration of training programmes, course materials and liaison between the training department and trainees all play an important part in producing effective training.

► CHAPTER REVIEW ◄

1. A training administrator's key tasks are:
   - To manage training administration
   - To assist in production of training materials
   - To select and book training venues and facilities

2. Training administration
Effective administration of training programmes, schedules, venues and course materials can ensure the success of training within the organization.

3. Training notes
All course handouts should be professionally presented – with the corporate logo on all handouts if possible.
   Training notes should follow the structure of the training session, and it is prudent for all trainers to be skilled in the art of writing training notes.

4. Training facilities
The selection of suitable training venues both in-house and outside the organization is a time-consuming yet important task. A checklist for itemizing, planning and organizing these facilities is essential.

9   **Selecting New Trainers**

▷   CHAPTER SUMMARY   ◁

A guide to the selection and recruitment of new trainers.
- Identify trainer qualities
- Define the job of trainer
- List required training methods, styles and strategies
- Conduct a performance appraisal
- Select and interview potential new trainers
- Shortlist candidates
- Make your final selection

Identify Trainer Qualities

A training department depends on the expertise and proficiency of its trainers. For the organization and its employees to achieve training targets, the trainers need to be selected and trained to the highest standards.

Before we can select new trainers, we must evaluate our current team of trainers. Refer to Chapter 6: 'The Training Team and their Skills'.

Activity

Many diverse qualities are expected from trainers. Devise your own list of the qualities your ideal training team possesses after studying the points below.

The ideal trainer is:
- Knowledgeable about the organization
- Informed about products, services and subject

- Technically competent
- Well-versed in interpersonal skills
- Committed to the organization
- Interested in the staff (and in people generally)
- Able to demonstrate excellent questioning techniques
- Able to listen carefully to others
- Able to communicate persuasively and effectively
- Able to analyse and solve problems

- Flexible in the use of training methods
- A conscientious time manager
- A competent planner and organizer
- A reliable administrator
- Qualified to balance a budget
- A clear, precise writer
- A clear, persuasive speaker
- Responsible for trainee performance and attitudes
- Able to show initiative and innovation
- Able to respond rather than react to situations
- Able to take time to listen intelligently

The list of required qualities may be very daunting to someone who is just starting out in training. Every trainer has strengths and weaknesses, and provided there are opportunities to develop trainer expertise within the organization, and the trainer is willing, weaknesses can be turned to strengths.

The following six steps are a guide to help you analyse your current training team, and to determine whether new trainers are required. Your list of ideal qualities will help you to identify the qualities you require from current and new trainers.

1. Define the job of trainer
2. List required training methods, styles and strategies
3. Conduct a performance appraisal
4. Select and interview potential new trainers
5. Shortlist candidates
6. Make your final selection

Define the Job of Trainer

This can be done in two stages:
Checklist – Ask all the trainers on your team to provide information

about their own jobs. This can be done in the form of a list of tasks and responsibilities currently fulfilled. A master checklist should then be compiled for analysis.

Brainstorming session – A brainstorming session with your entire training team will highlight areas of weakness in your team. A SWOT analysis will identify which tasks are fulfilled competently, and where there is room for improvement. It will also determine which skills may be required from a new trainer.

List Required Training Methods, Styles and Strategies

Analyse the training methods and training styles required within your organization. See Chapter 5 for definitions of training methods.

Training methods

Which methods are relevant to and needed by your trainers?

- Lecture or demonstration
- Participative lesson
- Individual coaching
- Tutor-led group discussion
- Role-playing
- Critical incident
- Training games
- Distance learning
- Computer-based training (CBT)
- Interactive video
- Self-teach training manual
- Case study
- On-job instruction
- Packaged programmes
- Programmed instruction
- Assignment, task or project

Training styles

The delivery of successful training programmes depends on the adoption of the right training style:

- Presenter
- Facilitator
- Leader
- Teacher
- Instructor
- Controller
- Negotiator

Training strategies

The delivery of successful training programmes depends on the right approach:

- Autocratic
- Didactic
- Positive
- Confident

- Enthusiastic
- Democratic
- Instructive

Conduct a Performance Appraisal

A more formal approach to assessing your team is the performance appraisal. A performance appraisal is a systematic assessment of an individual's performance, and can help to:

- Determine which skills expected of your current training team are not currently met
- Assess future training needs for your trainers

To conduct a performance appraisal, you will need to interview each trainer personally. To further evaluate their skills, attitudes and characteristics, you may need to:

- Analyse each trainer's job description and job specification
- Observe the trainer at work

During the appraisal, the following questions will highlight each trainer's potential. It will also identify which skills may be required from a new trainer:

- How has the job grown or changed since the trainer started with the organization?
- Will the role of trainer continue to change in the near future?
- What tasks and responsibilities does the trainer currently do well?
- What are the weaknesses of the trainer?
- What further training and experience does the trainer require?
- How does the trainer see the job developing?
- What new responsibilities is the trainer willing to adopt?
- How is the trainer perceived within the organization?

Select and Interview Potential New Trainers

Once you have defined the job of trainer, completed performance appraisals (optional), and identified current training methods, styles and strategies, you are in a position to assess what new trainers are required for your team. Completion of the following questionnaire will allow you to do just that:

- What are the tasks and responsibilities demanded of your current trainers?
- What knowledge and skills exist in the current training team?
- Which responsibilities are not satisfied within your present team?
- What skill gaps need to be filled?
- Which jobs are to be filled? (ie trainer, administrator, etc)
- How many posts are to be filled?
- What are the sum total of duties expected from new trainers?
- What training and development will be available to new training staff?
- Who else should be involved in this selection process?

Activity
- Which qualities are you looking for in a new trainer?
  Do you want them to:
    - Design relevant quality programmes?
    - Motivate other trainers and employees?
    - Help delegates enjoy their training?
    - Be competent and experienced trainers?
- Make a list of the qualities expected from current trainers.
- Delete any items which are irrelevant for a new trainer.
- Add whichever tasks, roles, functions, duties or responsibilities are to be expected from a new recruit to the training team.

This assessment will help you to prepare the Job Description (what the job is) for the new trainer, and the Job Specification (qualities needed to fulfil the job description).

To conduct a selection interview

Three factors will ensure a successful and well structured interview:

1. Prepare thoroughly

2. Allow the candidate sufficient opportunity to talk and ask questions
3. Communicate the key aspects of the job

1. Prepare thoroughly
   - Know the job description and job specification
   - Analyse the application form
   - Plan the shape of the interview
   - Consider the information the candidate wants to know
2. Allow the candidate sufficient opportunity to talk and ask questions

Personal contact at the start of the interview is important. Devote the first five minutes to helping the candidate to relax.

The next thirty minutes are exploratory. Encourage the candidate to speak by asking clear, precise questions which begin with the following words: who, what, why, where, when, which and how.

These questions identify specific aspects of a candidate's qualifications, attitudes, strengths and weaknesses. Ask questions about their current or previous job, attitudes to their company, personal attitudes to training and management, previous successes, failures, lessons learned, suitability for the job, and personal values. For example:

   - What were your responsibilities in your previous job?
   - Why are you looking for a new position?
   - What attracts you to this job? to this company?
   - What do you feel is the main purpose of the job?
   - How do you feel about training?
   - What do you feel you can bring to this department?
   - How successful are you in your current job?
   - What areas are you most proud of? least proud of?
   - What are your ambitions?
   - Which part of your work do you most enjoy?
   - How would you describe your personality?

3. Communicate the key aspects of the job

Communicate the job specification (in outline) and its benefits to the candidate. Enough information should be provided by the interviewer about the organization, its products and services, the job position and responsibilities.

This will motivate the candidate and promote discussion. Discussion will help to confirm whether the candidate is suitable and qualified.

Shortlist Candidates

On completion of candidate interviews, shortlist the personnel best suited to the new role.

An assessment of the candidates, how they handled the job interview, and the relevance of their abilities to the training post in question will help decide which candidates should be considered for final selection.

Activity – How to Prepare a Shortlist

1. To prepare your shortlist, compile a list of the skills and characteristics of each candidate interviewed. Divide this list into two columns: strengths and weaknesses.

Evaluate these strengths and weaknesses against the job specification and job description prepared for the new recruit.

2. Draft a second list which places each candidate into a Must, Should or Could category. In other words, are they a *must* for the post, *should* they be chosen because they are well suited to the post, or *could* they simply fulfil the basic requirements of the job? Helpful hints:

Automatically eliminate candidates who do not satisfy the selection requirements, and try to keep your *must* list to three candidates.

3. Prioritize the *must* list and evaluate the skills and characteristics of those chosen candidates to make your final selection.

Trainer's Tip

Remember that the key aspects of a trainer's role within the organization are to:

- Provide a service to the organization
- Offer support and guidance to management
- Work closely with management to achieve organizational objectives
- Identify and satisfy training needs

Make Your Final Selection

With your shortlist in hand, make a note of the skills or characteristics which are not satisfied in the new personnel, and decide whether these can be met within your current training team. If not, it may be a case of training both current and new personnel in whatever fresh skills, attitudes or knowledge you have specified.

To confirm the decision to recruit new trainers, develop your existing team, or both, the checklist below will offer a final evaluation of your needs.

CHECKLIST

1. What skills are lacking in your training department?
2. Which training methods, styles and strategies need to be incorporated into your training sessions?
3. What training needs are not satisfied by your current team?
4. Can a new trainer satisfy these needs, or should you consider training your existing team?
5. What skills should a new trainer bring into the training department?

Conclusion

Prior to interviewing and selecting new trainers, it is important to determine what qualities will be expected of a new recruit, and what skills or performance gaps exist in your current training team.

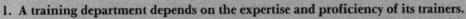

CHAPTER REVIEW

1. A training department depends on the expertise and proficiency of its trainers.
2. A prerequisite to selecting and recruiting new trainers is to analyse the skills and performance of your current team.
3. Six steps will help you decide whether you should recruit new staff to strengthen your existing training team.
   - Define the job of trainer in the organization
   - List required training methods, styles and strategies
   - Conduct a performance appraisal (optional)
   - Select and interview new trainers
   - Shortlist the best candidates
   - Make your final decision
4. The performance appraisal is a useful assessment of your current trainers and can help to determine which skills are not currently met, and to assess future trainer needs.
5. After shortlisting candidates, determine which required skills are now met by current and new trainers.

10 Training – An Investment in the Organization

▷   **CHAPTER SUMMARY**   ◁

This chapter looks at validation of training activities as a measurement of trainee job performance.

- Training is an excellent investment
- Validation and evaluation
- Validating the effects of training

Training is an Excellent Investment

All organizations would like to see a return on their investment in training. Training is an investment in your personnel, and an investment in your staff is an investment in your organization.

Staff who are motivated and happy are likely to stay longer with the company, so turnover is reduced. Competent and well-trained staff perform better, work more efficiently, and are therefore more likely to achieve organizational goals and increase company profits.

We invest in equipment, so why not in people? Every organization invests in capital equipment and materials to maintain performance targets and increase profits. That is no different from investing in personnel to maintain and develop their skills. Individual performance within the organization affects overall profit.

Validation and Evaluation

To calculate a return on training we need to:

- Validate training activities
- Evaluate the financial worth of training activities

Validation: this is the practical measurement of a trainee's job performance (post-training) in the application of knowledge, skills and attitudes. There are two types of validation: internal and external.

1. Internal validation: assesses whether a training activity has achieved its objectives.
2. External validation: assesses whether the trainees have applied their learning in the workplace.

Evaluation: this assesses the total financial worth of training to the organization and the individual employee.

Evaluation is concerned with assessing the benefits of training in financial terms to the organization. This includes training costs and the influence of improved job performance on profitability.

The training department is no different from any other department within an organization in that it should yield measurable benefits and profits. Individual trainees receive benefits from training, and those benefits should be translated into:

- Improved job performance
- Increased profits for the organization

Validating the effects of training

To validate the success of the training function we need to assess training on two levels – the organization and the individual. In this chapter we will examine the effects of training on the organization. We can assess:

- The purpose of current training activities
- The training benefit to the organization
- Whether all training objectives are being met.

The purpose of current training activities

Training provides management with professional support to meet organizational objectives; this is true whether training is an integral part of the personnel function, or a department in its own right.

Although trainers bring many skills to the organization, the final responsibility for training rests with the line manager or supervisor. The co-operation between trainer, line manager and trainee will determine the success of training activities within the organization.

Reviewing your training objectives, policies and strategies in the light of organizational objectives, policies and strategies enables you to:

- Appraise whether training objectives are being met
- Survey the training methods used
- Assess how training is applied in the workplace

Are your trainers using the right methods, styles and strategies to achieve your training objectives? Remember, your training objectives and policies should mirror those of the organization.

The training benefit to the organization

A post-training audit for each trainee is one of the best ways to calculate the effects of training, and to survey how training is being applied in the workplace.

Training has an impact on key performance areas which affect profitability. A post-training audit (sometimes called a performance analysis) can identify:

- How performance has improved due to training
- How this performance can be quantified
- Which training activities have proved most effective in enhancing performance
- How improved performance has reduced costs
- What new training is required

Are all training objectives being met?

To ensure training objectives are met for each training session, a number of methods can be used:

- pre-course briefing
- personal goals statement
- the training contract
- course evaluation
- post-training debrief
- post-training audit
- performance appraisal

> Bearing in mind the course objectives as outlined by the trainer, my personal goals for this course are:
> 1. To gain a better understanding of the concepts of marketing
> 2. To reflect on how marketing works in my organization
> 3. To relate marketing concepts to my role as a sales executive

Figure 10.1 *Personal Goals Statement*

Pre-course briefing: prior to any course, the trainee should be given an effective pre-course briefing to discuss the purpose of attending the training programme, and to demonstrate commitment to the training objectives and a post-course action plan.

Personal goals statement: at the start of each training activity, the trainer sets out the specific objectives for the course and outlines the benefits to be gained.

Each trainee should be asked to write down several personal goals which the training is expected to fulfill. This is sometimes called an objectives statement: it indicates the trainee's objectives for the course. An example is given in Figure 10.1 from a trainee who attended a course on the basics of marketing principles.

The training contract: this reconciles the trainer's objectives for the training programme with those of individual trainees. It requires an exercise which can take 30–60 minutes and involves an analysis and reconciliation of trainer and trainee expectations.

The primary benefit of this exercise is to prevent a trainee misunderstanding the reasons for attending the course, which can cause hostility or disappointment.

The role of the trainer

A way of reaching an understanding between trainer and trainees about the objectives for the training session is to conduct an open discussion with the group. Invite the trainees to express the roles and functions they expect of the trainer. The trainer notes these items on a flip chart.

The trainer then explains his/her own previously prepared set of roles and functions for that training session. The two lists should be compared and reconciled by the group and the trainer.

The role of the trainee

The same procedure can be completed for the role of the trainee. The trainer and each trainee devise individual lists of the roles and functions expected from the trainees. Using the flip chart, the trainees and tutor reconcile their lists.

Discussion questions

This is a tutor-led discussion:

1. What do the trainees expect from the session that the trainer does not intend to provide at this time?
2. What is the reason for these expectations?
3. What does the trainer intend to provide that was not expected by the trainees?
4. What problems, if any, do the trainees anticipate in reconciling their expectations with the trainer's?
5. What can be done to prevent problems due to irreconcilable expectations?

Feedback sessions, group discussions and individual tutorials during the course will provide many opportunities for the trainer to establish how trainees are responding to the training.

Course evaluation:

Trainee statement

At the end of a training session, each trainee should note what benefits were personally gained from the training activities, and evaluate which training objectives (identified at the start of the course) were met. This should be shared with the group in an open discussion. The example below was a contribution from a young personal assistant (PA) at the end of a one-day course on publicity.

Trainee statement
1. What I have gained for myself:
   - Confidence and faith in my own abilities
   - The skills to design and write a press release
   - The understanding of why I should produce a workable media contact list
2. What I plan to do differently on my return to work
   - Sit down with my manager to agree an action plan
   - Build in planning and production time for my new publicity activities

---

Course evaluation questionnaire

Feedback at the end of a training programme is important to trainees, trainers and line managers. This type of feedback can be done quite simply in the form of a one-page questionnaire. Enough time should be designated at the end of the course. This will guarantee that the information given is complete and well thought out. Allow 20–30 minutes for trainees to fill in the questionnaire, with a follow-up discussion.

> **Trainer's Tip**
> The trainer's reactions to the trainees is a fundamental aspect of the validation process. During a training session, a trainer will be constantly aware of the performance of individual trainees. This is important feedback to be discussed with the line manager.

The questionnaire should ask:

- How relevant were the training objectives to the trainee's job?
- What value was the programme content to the delegates?
- How much of the subject matter was new?
- Were the training methods effective?
- Were the presentation and communication skills of the trainer competent?
- What could be done differently to improve the course?

It is valuable for these points to be shared in a tutor-led group discussion. An example of a course evaluation questionnaire is shown in Figure 10.2.

Course evaluation questionnaires are crucial to evaluate the positive and negative aspects of a training session. They indicate where and how the course content, timings and handouts need changing or fine-tuning. The questionnaires can also be used as a basis for discussion during the debriefing session between trainees and line managers.

Post-training debrief: as a follow-up to the course, it is important that the trainees are debriefed by their immediate supervisor or line manager. It is then the responsibility of the supervisor or line manager to assess the individual's performance in the workplace as a result of the training. This may take the form of a post-training audit or a regular performance appraisal.

Post-training audit: a post-training audit identifies changes in job performance or job behaviour which are a result of training. It shows whether the training gap has been closed: this is known as the transfer of learning.

> **Trainer's Tip**
> Transfer of learning refers to whether the job performance gap has been closed. If the trainee has not successfully transferred the

Name: Course title:
Job title: Course venue:
Department: Course dates:
                                           Course Tutor:

We take training very seriously in our organization. To help us provide training programmes which are of maximum benefit to you, we would appreciate it if you would reflect on the training programme you have just completed. Please circle the answer which most applies to you.

1. Were the course objectives clearly explained?
    Completely, Very well, Fairly well, Not at all
2. Were the course objectives relevant to your individual needs?
    Completely, Very well, Fairly well, Not at all
3. Was the subject matter relevant to your job needs?
    Completely, Very well, Fairly well, Not at all
4. Was the content of the course logically structured?
    Completely, Very well, Fairly well, Not at all
5. Were the methods of training relevant to the course content?
    Completely, Very well, Fairly well, Not at all
6. Were you encouraged to participate?
    Completely, Very well, Fairly well, Not at all
7. Did the trainer handle the visual aids well?
    Completely, Very well, Fairly well, Not at all
8. Were the course handouts useful and relevant to the course content?
    Completely, Very well, Fairly well, Not at all
9. Will the course handouts be of help to you in the future?
    Completely, Very well, Fairly well, Not at all
10. Was the trainer's presentation of the course of a high standard?
    Completely, Very well, Fairly Well, Not at all
11. Was the training environment conducive to learning and comfortable?
    Completely, Very well, Fairly well, Not at all
12. Were the assignments and exercises of practical benefit?
    Completely, Very well, Fairly well, Not at all
13. Did the trainer offer individual support and guidance to you?
    Completely, Very well, Fairly well, Not at all
14. Will you be able to apply what you have learned on the course in the workplace?
    Completely, Very well, Fairly well, Not at all
15. If you could change anything on the course, what would you change? _____

_____

_____

Figure 10.2 *Course evaluation questionnaire*

required knowledge, skills, or behaviour to the job, it may be necessary to examine the effectiveness of the training, or the suitability of the training techniques and methods used.

Following training three questions should be asked:

1. Has the trainee learned effectively?
2. What learning has the trainee retained?
3. How easy was the transfer of learning from the training environment to the work environment?

If too long a gap ensues after the training session and before the training audit, there is a possibility that the work environment may interfere with determining what was learned in direct training.

Performance appraisal: it should be possible for a post-training audit to follow the debriefing session between the line manager and the trainee. If not, the next occasion for an assessment of job performance will be the regular performance appraisal. See Chapter 18.

Conclusion

Internal validation assesses whether a training activity has achieved its objectives, and external validation assesses whether the trainees have applied their learning in the workplace. In this chapter we examined validation and the effects of training on the organization.

▶ **CHAPTER REVIEW** ◀

1. Training is an investment in any organization for two reasons:
   - Motivated and happy staff stay longer and staff turnover is reduced
   - Competent and well-trained staff perform better, work more efficiently, and are more likely to achieve organizational goals
2. Validation is the measurement of a trainee's job performance in terms of application of knowledge, skills and attitudes post-training. Validation assesses:
   - Whether a training activity has achieved its objectives
   - Whether the trainees have applied their learning in the workplace
3. Evaluation is the term used to assess the total financial worth of training in terms of costs and benefits to the organization and the employee.
4. To validate training for the organization we should:
   - Ask whether training objectives are being met
   - Assess the training methods used
   - Assess how training is being applied in the work place
5. To determine if training objectives are being met for each activity requires a combination of actions:
   - pre-course briefing
   - personal goals statement
   - the training contract
   - course evaluation
   - post-training debrief
   - post-training audit
   - performance appraisal

11 Evaluating the Cost-benefits of Training

$\triangleright$ **CHAPTER SUMMARY** $\triangleleft$

- Evaluating the cost-benefits of training for the organization
- Monitoring and controlling the training budget
- Training cost analysis

Evaluation is an assessment of the total worth of training to the organization and the individual employee. In this chapter we examine different methods of evaluating training and its cost-benefits for the organization.

Evaluating the Cost-benefits of Training for the Organization

To evaluate the financial costs of the training function, we need to ask:

- What are the on-going financial costs required to manage the training department?
- How can we assess the financial significance of the training delivered?

What are the on-going financial costs?

A training department is similar to any other department within the organization; monetary costs are needed for resources. These may include:

- Office and administrative costs
- Staff salaries, wages and expenses
- Training development costs
- Cost of new equipment
- Depreciation of old equipment and maintenance costs
- Cost to hire training equipment and venues
- Space occupation costs
- Course costs for trainee and trainer materials
- Travel and subsistence costs for trainees and trainers
- Fees and expenses for external trainers

How can we assess the financial significance of the training delivered?

Training objectives indicate what results are expected from a training session. Therefore training can be related specifically to expected trainee outcomes or results.

As discussed earlier, a post-training audit can assess the results of the training undergone. The significant areas where change is expected and which will indicate whether the money spent on training was well spent are:

- Acquisition and application of knowledge
  - What new knowledge has been acquired?
- Skills acquisition
  - Has the trainee acquired new skills or improved current skills?
- Changes in attitude and behaviour
  - What changes have there been in individual behaviour and attitude?

To evaluate the significance of training in financial terms we need to compare the money spent on training, cost savings due to improved performance, and the financial benefits the organization has received due to training. The following questions are a guideline:

1. What cost savings are expected from improved employee job performance?
2. What benefits does the organization expect to see post-training?
3. How do these benefits relate to the money spent on training in the organization?

It can often be difficult to quantify the significance of training. If trainee performance has been improved, areas of advancement can be specified in relation to the above three categories, with particular reference to cost savings due to improved performance and perceived benefits to the organization.

Benefits may be concentrated in several areas; for example: improved sales, improved profitability, enhanced customer satisfaction, improved product performance, better customer care, greater safety and hygiene in the work environment, and more confident, positive employee attitudes.

Monitoring and Controlling the Training Budget

Budget categories

Control of the budget is achieved by regular checking that expenditure does not exceed allotted finances. Who has responsibility for the budget, and who has final authorization of expenditure?

It is advisable to exercise control by dividing the budget into manageable categories. To forecast the training budget we need to estimate how much money should be allocated to each category.

Separate categories may be allocated for: salaries, wages and expenses; purchase and hire of training equipment; production and purchase of training materials; travel and accommodation expenses for trainees and trainers; fees and expenses for external consultants, etc.

Fixed and variable costs

Every organization has its fixed and variable costs, and the training department will be no exception.

Fixed costs remain constant whether or not you increase sales, or produce and deliver new training programmes. These are costs such as capital investment in the building, rent, business rates, insurance, salaries and wages, heating, lighting, cleaning, telephones, photocopying, postage and stationery.

Variable costs are normally incurred during manufacture or distribution and vary by the volume produced. In training terms, variable costs will be incurred in relation to the number of training programmes you produce and deliver.

These variable costs include development of course materials, overtime, research and development, promotion costs, the hire of external training venues and the recruitment of external consultants.

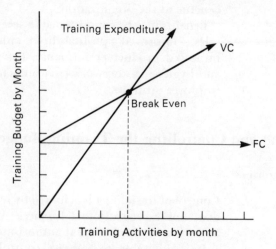

FC = Fixed Costs, VC = Variable Costs
Break Even = Point where costs break even with budget

Figure 11.1 *Fixed and Variable Costs*

These costs should be carefully monitored as they vary month to month according to your training activities.

Fixed and variable costs are usually determined in relation to sales revenue. The difficulty with training is that there is no obvious income incurred from training. What can be assessed is the impact of training on performance, although it is not always possible to show this immediately in terms of increased sales or increased profit. But fixed and variable costs can be compared to training expenditure to show how the money has been spent.

Figure 11.1 illustrates these two sets of costs in relation to the training budget and training expenditure. It can help you determine if and how you are overspending your training budget.

Return on Investment (ROI)

In many organizations, training is considered to be an expenditure with no obvious return on investment. However, a return on investment is clearly reflected in improved performance and/or increased profit.

Return on investment (ROI) is sometimes called the rate of return (ROR). In training terms ROI measures the financial improvement in performance, and cost savings achieved from training activities.

Example

In a retail manufacturing unit, sales training was undertaken by the field sales representatives, and time management training was undertaken by the sales managers.

It was expected that the sales training would increase unit sales by the sales representatives. The time management training improved sales management delegation of tasks, organization skills and left more effective time for planning.

In financial terms, the success of this training could be expressed in terms of profitability by the sales representatives, and savings in staff overtime due to better time management and delegation of tasks by the sales managers.

Financial statement

An end of year financial statement is a means of organizing and presenting the training accounts for the internal analysis of management, and as a report to shareholders.

At the end of the financial year, your department should produce a financial statement which indicates the level of training expenditure over the year. This includes how the money was used to develop and maintain a skilled and efficient workforce.

The format for financial information will be explained by your accounts and finance department. It may take the form of a balance sheet which shows the training department's source and application of funds, and the department's performance over the financial year.

The various items included in your financial statement may be:

- Fixed costs
- Variable costs
- Value of paid and unpaid invoices

- New equipment purchased
- Depreciation of old equipment
- Storage costs

- Costs of all training activities

- Costs of producing new training courses
- Savings due to improved performance
- Anticipated future costs

Training Cost Analysis

To measure the cost of training we can evaluate four types of costs:

1. Total costs to manage the training function
2. Overall training costs per day
3. Internal trainer costs per day
4. Cost benefit analysis

Total costs to manage the training function

The combination of fixed and variable costs should be analysed each month or financial quarter. The total fixed and variable costs in a twelve-month financial period equals the annual cost to manage the training department. The equation is:

Fixed costs + variable costs = Total training costs

If your fixed costs for a twelve-month period represent a sum total of £48,000, and your variable costs represent a total of £24,000, your total training costs for the financial year total £72,000.

£48,000 (fixed) + £24,000 (variable) = £72,000 (annual)

£72,000 ÷ 12 = £6,000 (monthly average)

The average monthly cost is arrived at by dividing by 12 months. This produces £6,000 as an average monthly cost for all training activities. This will help you to evaluate what costs will be required for the next financial year.

Overall training costs per day

To calculate the average cost of a training day, divide the annual cost of training by the total number of days worked in the organization in the year. If the annual cost is £72,000 and the number of training days is 250, the cost of managing the training department is £288 per day.

$$\frac{£72,000 \text{ (annual cost of training)}}{250 \text{ (total number of days worked)}} = £288 \text{ (per day)}$$

> **Trainer's Tip**
> An excellent analysis of managing training costs is to be found in Rosemary Harrison's *Training and Development* (1991).

Internal trainer costs per day

To calculate the daily cost of employing your internal team of trainers, use the following calculation. Divide the annual training cost by the total number of days worked by your trainers. If you have two trainers who have worked 200 days each, that is a total of 400 days.

$$\frac{\text{Total training costs for the year}}{\text{Total number of days trainers worked}} = \text{Daily trainer costs}$$

$$\frac{£72,000}{400} = £180 \text{ (per day)}$$

This calculation is essential when analysing the cost to recruit an external training consultant. It allows you to measure the cost of an outside consultant against the average daily cost of your internal trainers.

Cost-benefit analysis

A cost-benefit analysis compares the cost of training to the benefits expected to be received from training.

The organization is usually looking for benefits in terms of improved job performance and increased profits. To conduct a cost-benefit analysis these two questions should be answered:

- What improvement is there in job performance due to training?
- In what way have profits increased following training?

Expected benefits may mean improved costs per unit of production, improved quality control, or a reduction in cost per order taken. A record of unit production costs (or costs per order) can be kept pre-training and post-training. Quality control may be evaluated by monitoring (pre- and post-training) the number of complaints from customers and the quantity and value of faulty goods produced.

Conclusion

In this chapter we examined the process of evaluating training. Evaluation is an assessment of the financial significance of training, selecting the right method to monitor and control the training budget, and an analysis of the costs and benefits of training.

▶   **CHAPTER REVIEW**   ◀

1. To evaluate the financial costs of the training function we need to ask:
   - What are the on-going financial costs?
   - How can we assess the financial significance of the training delivered?

2. An analysis of the significance of training in financial terms requires a comparison of:
   - cost savings due to improved performance
   - post-training benefits to the organization
   - how benefits relate to money spent on training

3. Methods used to monitor and control the training budget are:
   - separate budget categories
   - fixed and variable costs
   - return on investment (ROI)
   - financial statement

4. A training cost analysis calculates:
   - Total costs to manage the training function
   - Internal trainer costs per day
   - Overall training costs per day
   - Cost benefit analysis

12 An Investment in the Individual

> **CHAPTER SUMMARY** ◁

- An investment in individual performance
- Monitoring post-training job performance
- How the individual affects profits
- Neglected areas of training

An Investment in Individual Performance

The implications for training have been examined in terms of validating and evaluating job performance at the organizational level. The credibility of the training function should be assessed on an individual level as well as that of the organization.

Reliable feedback on individual performance will help the training department to regularly improve the design and delivery of training to satisfy individual and organizational needs. Investment in the individual can be examined by asking:

- Has training improved individual performance?
- How is improved performance supervised and monitored?
- What impact has individual performance had on profitability?
- Have neglected areas of training affected performance and profit?

Has training improved performance?

All good training should produce benefits to the individual at the level of knowledge, skills or behaviour. The trainer's job is to:

- Help identify training objectives within the organization
- Explain and communicate the benefits of training to management
- Deliver effective training programmes to satisfy individual and organizational needs

Training will be wasted if it does not address:

Performance: The organization's need to improve work performance and achieve organizational targets.
Growth: The employee's need for personal growth and development.
Needs: The trainer's ability to identify individual needs and organizational needs.

Monitoring Post-training Job Performance

To assess the impact of training on individual performance, enhanced personal development and needs, three types of evaluation can be carried out:

1. End of course evaluation by the trainee
2. Trainer's evaluation of the trainee
3. Line manager's evaluation of trainee performance

End of course evaluation by the trainee

The trainee completes the end of course questionnaire which can be used as a group discussion tool. It is valuable as a guide in the debriefing session that takes place between line manager and trainee. It provides valuable information for the trainer regarding:

- Individual training needs which have been satisfied
- Learning that took place during training
- Subject matter which was not relevant to the needs of the trainees on the course

See the course evaluation questionnaire, Figure 10.2, page 100.

Trainer's evaluation of the trainee

During a training session the trainer is able to make an assessment of trainee behaviour. This includes how well the trainee participated in the training activities and discussions, and to some extent what knowledge and skills were acquired by the end of the training session.

Appropriate feedback on trainee performance can also be passed on to line managers in the form of a course report. This will help trainers and line managers to plan future developmental training.

It is important that your team of trainers regularly meets for a debriefing session. These practical sessions should fit easily into the trainers' schedules and may be daily, weekly or monthly.

The results of these debriefing sessions should be recorded. These records are useful tools to monitor changes to training strategy.

Activity
Listed below are principal items to be discussed in a trainer's debriefing session. What other topics would you add to the list?
- Trainee reactions at the end of the course
- Overall performance of trainees during training
- Success in achieving course training objectives

- Review of session structure, content and methodology
- Pre-course organization and administration
- Analysis of trainer's own performance

- Changes required to course content, structure or methodology to meet changing needs

- Points of action
- Allocation of responsibility

Line manager's evaluation of trainee performance

The trainee's immediate line manager is the ideal person in the organization to assess the trainee's post-training job performance and behaviour. This is where a trainer's course report can be invaluable.

The line manager will also be able to judge how the training programme has influenced the trainee compared with other influences in the work environment.

The line manager and trainee should discuss three main topics as a follow-up to training. They are:

- Positive performance targets agreed prior to the course

- The trainee's action points drawn up at the end of the training session
- The method of post-training audit to assess the knowledge, skills and behaviour gained

Positive performance targets: Prior to attendance on a training course, it is important for the line manager and trainee to agree positive performance targets which will be the result of training. These may have been agreed previously in a performance appraisal, or may be agreed at the pre-course briefing. The trainer should be informed of these targets.

Action plan: An action plan drawn up by the trainee at the end of the training session will indicate which actions will be implemented upon returning to work. These action points should be shared with the line manager during the post-training debriefing session. The action plan should be followed up by the line manager.

Post-training audit: There are several ways for the manager to assess if the trainee has gained the targeted knowledge, skills and behaviour. This may be through a post-training audit which can take different forms depending on the job and individual.

A post-training audit assesses how training has been applied on the job. This type of audit can take several forms:

- A supervised trainee action plan
- A knowledge or skills test (written or oral)
- Discussion of the end-of-course questionnaire
- A follow-up interview
- Direct on-job observation
- A supervised special project
- A regular performance appraisal

These methods are analysed in greater detail in Chapter 13. Their main purpose is to reappraise:

- The fulfilment of training needs
- The application of learning in the workplace
- Improvements or changes in job performance

How is improved performance supervised and monitored?

It is the ultimate responsibility of the line manager to supervise the performance of an employee. However, the trainer should be involved in this process as a support and guide to the line manager. Monitoring individual performance can be accomplished if there is a structured approach to:

- The analysis of job tasks and responsibilities
- A post-training audit system
- A performance appraisal system which is formally linked to the training function
- Clearly set targets which are regularly reviewed

Trainer's Tip
To be most effective, course training objectives should be in line with targets which are regularly set and reviewed.
New training objectives should be set, when appropriate, for each course and used as a tool to improve performance.

How the Individual affects Profits

An organization is made up of the individuals who work for it. Without a fully trained work force, an organization will not be able to perform to designated standards, and will not be in a position to increase profits. The organization requires the highest standards from its employees to achieve success and improve profitability.

The individual influences organizational profit because:

1. All revenue and profit is made by the organization's employees
2. Employees who are well trained and motivated operate at maximum performance level
3. Training plays a major role in assessing and fulfilling organizational needs and individual needs

What impact has individual performance had on profitability?

To achieve maximum performance levels, reduce costs, and increase profitability an estimate should be made of:

- How many people are required to run the business profitably and efficiently?
- What abilities do individuals require to perform satisfactorily in the market place?
- How can individuals be motivated and developed for the good of the organization?
- How can the individual within the organization cope

effectively with changes in society and in the market-place and still perform to standard?

● What training is required to improve individual performance and manage the work force profitably?

Example

Training dramatically improved performance and company profitability in a regional newspaper sales department. A newspaper sales executive, who had undergone intensive sales training, was expected to increase unit sales of newspapers to key trade accounts. This executive's key trade accounts were major multiple newsagents responsible for sales of daily newspapers.

A pre- and post-training performance audit was administered to analyse any change in this particular representative's unit sales. Following training, the sales executive increased his monthly unit sales by 5 per cent each month over a six-month period. This had an immediate effect on newspaper sales and profitability.

To calculate the representative's sales performance, a record was kept of his pre-training sales to major multiple newsagents, compared with two separate, three-month periods following training. National economic factors and seasonal trends which affected the newspaper industry in those six months were taken into account.

The entire department's sales team was appraised in the same manner to determine what effect training had on overall newspaper sales to major multiple newsagents, and if the improvement in sales affected profitability.

Neglected Areas of Training

Some areas of training may have been overlooked in the organization. This may be due to limited resources, ie only a finite number of trainers and training programmes are available within the organization.

Have neglected areas of training affected performance and profit?

To determine which areas of training have been neglected, review organizational and individual training needs. Then analyse what training is required to close the gap and improve performance, and determine what effect this will have on profitability.

Activity

Which areas of training need to be developed to close the gap and ensure performance objectives are met? Your plan of action requires research in five areas:

1. To review organizational training needs
2. To review individual training needs
3. To assess which needs are not currently satisfied by training
4. What training is required to improve performance?
5. What effect will this new training have on profit?

Conclusion

In this chapter we looked at the impact the individual has on organizational performance and profitability. If performance objectives are not met, this will obviously have a serious effect on profit.

Reliable feedback on individual performance will help the training department to design and deliver training to close the gap between current and required performance.

▶ **CHAPTER REVIEW** ◀

1. Individual performance can have a significant impact on profitability. This is because revenue and profits are made by the organization's employees. They will perform at maximum performance level if they are well trained and motivated.

2. An assessment of the training on individual performances can be divided into three areas:
   - End of course evaluation
   - Trainer evaluation of the trainee
   - Line manager evaluation of trainee performance

3. To ensure trainees have gained the targeted knowledge, skills and behaviour:
   - Positive performance targets must be set
   - A post-training action plan should be implemented
   - A post-training audit should be undertaken

4. The line manager is ultimately responsible for the supervision and monitoring of improved job performance on the part of the trainee.
   The trainer plays a role by sharing appropriate feedback on individual trainee performance and participation during a training session.

5. The function of a post-training audit is to:
   - Determine fulfilment of training needs
   - Survey application of learning in the workplace
   - Note any changes in job performance

13 Monitoring and Reporting Results

▷   CHAPTER SUMMARY   ◁

Four areas enable us to monitor and report the results of training:
- Achievement of training objectives
- Transfer of learning to the work environment
- Methods of evaluating training effectiveness
- Responsibility for monitoring and reporting

Achievement of Training Objectives

Measuring and proving results is the area of training which gives most trainers a headache! However, there are several ways of looking at what is actually achieved from training for individual employees and the organization.

This is accomplished by validating whether the training session has achieved its objectives, appraising the transfer of learning to the work environment, and using the appropriate methods to evaluate post-training performance.

- What were the set objectives?
- Has the training session achieved its objectives?
- Did the trainees gain the knowledge or skills they were taught?

Example

A computer sales organization expected to increase sales with a new promotion to current and potential customers. They expected customers to telephone in response to a direct mail-shot. The mail-shot was designed to promote a new 0800 number. This new number enabled customers to place orders simply and easily by credit card over the phone.

Objectives set

As this had never been done before, the telephone sales team needed immediate training. The objectives were to learn how to handle calls positively, quickly and efficiently; to note all the relevant customer details and arrange for a follow-up call where required.

Achieved objectives

To measure the results of the training, the tele-sales supervisor needed coaching in 'on-job' observation techniques in order to supervise how the team handled the calls once they had undergone training.

What was gained?

To assess what was gained overall from the training sessions the following steps were taken:

Calls were quantified and orders were taken: results were measured by recording the number of calls made, and the number of orders taken on a daily, weekly and monthly basis. The number of sales to credit card holders versus regular retail customers were analysed, and the number of orders taken as a direct result of training were assessed.

Review session: a second method of assessment was to tape sample calls which were played back and commented on constructively during a post-training review session.

Transfer of Learning to the Work Environment

We need to evaluate the trainee's performance and application of skills upon return to the working environment.

- Have the trainees applied their new-found knowledge or skills to their job role?
- What improvement was expected after training?
- Has the trainee's performance improved to the level expected?

In Chapter 12 we examined the importance of post-training debriefing sessions between line manager and trainee, and monitoring post-training job performance.

Example

A young medical representative was recently sent on a one-day course (external to the organization) to learn how to demonstrate and sell anti-thromboid stockings to clinics and hospitals.

The main incentive for this training was an increase in salary if she successfully sold the anti-thromboid stockings.

Application of new skills

The medical representative attended a debriefing meeting with her line manager upon return to work and an action plan was agreed.

Over the next six months the representative spent 25 per cent of her time demonstrating the use of the anti-thromboid stockings to nursing staff in clinics and hospitals.

Improvement expected after training

Training objectives were set with the medical representative's line manager prior to the training course.

They were to:

- Learn the advantages and practical application of anti-thromboid stockings
- Increase her confidence in selling the product
- Increase her sales performance

Improved trainee performance

The results after six months indicated that the medical representative had successfully undertaken this new responsibility. The transfer of learning to the work environment was exceptional. Her sales of the new product exceeded all expectations and she was recommended for a salary increase.

Methods of Evaluating Training Effectiveness

Several methods can be used. All but the post-training audit and performance appraisal have been previously examined in detail:

- pre-course briefing
- the training contract
- end-of-course evaluation
- post-course debriefing
- post-training audit
- performance appraisal

The post-training audit: this is a vital ingredient in the training appraisal process. Its purpose is to evaluate the effectiveness of training in terms of the trainee's application of knowledge, skills and behaviour.

The primary types of post-training audit are:

- Trainee action plan
- Testing
- Post-course questionnaire
- A follow-up interview
- Direct on-job observation
- A supervised special project
- A regular performance appraisal

Trainee action plan

An action plan is a list of commitments which the trainee draws up in order of importance. The best time to write up an action plan is at the end of the training session, just before completion of the end of course questionnaire.

The action plan should be related to the training objectives explained by the tutor and agreed by the trainees at the start of the course. The points to be covered in an action plan are:

- An assessment of what the individual already does well
- What new skills have been learned on the course
- Key areas of improvement
- What will be done differently upon return to the work environment
- How training will improve performance

Example

1. What I already do well in my job position
2. Two things I have personally gained on the course which are relevant to my job role
3. The key areas in which I need to improve to increase job competence
4. What I will do differently when I return to the work environment to improve my job performance

5. What I need to do to ensure I continue to improve in my performance at work

A trainee action plan should be discussed with the line manager at a post-training debriefing session.

As a follow-up to the action plan, the line manager and trainee should meet after an agreed period to appraise what action has or has not been implemented. The trainer should liaise with the line manager to determine:

- If the action plan has been implemented
- How much of the action plan has been executed
- What knowledge, skills and behaviour have been used consistently
- What action steps have not been taken and why

Testing

The purpose of testing is to measure a trainee's acquisition of knowledge or skills, and to measure the effect of changes on job behaviour in the work environment.

Tests are considered to be a reliable and valid device with which to measure performance. They indicate the quantity or quality of work produced, and focus on the outcome of training in two major areas: an increase in knowledge and improved skills ability.

There are three main disadvantages to testing as a method of evaluating post-training performance.

1. A test or exam can be counter-productive to the learning environment set up in a training situation.
2. Testing places the trainee under a certain amount of stress, which is exactly what the training environment is trying to eliminate.
3. It is easier to test acquisition of knowledge or skills that are a result of training rather than changes in behaviour.

To be of most benefit, tests should be administered before a training course and on completion of the course as a comparison.

The primary advantages of testing are to measure the learning achieved from training, identify gaps in learning, and evaluate the individual's ability to learn in a training situation.

There are two major types of test: the performance test and the knowledge or skills test:

1. The performance test measures an individual's proficiency in applying knowledge, performing a skill, solving a problem, or demonstrating an aptitude for learning.

2. The knowledge or skills test (written or oral) seeks to examine the memory retention by the trainee on a particular subject.

Written tests

Written tests may take the form of multiple choice, matching lists, true-false statements or open questions:

Multiple choice: The multiple choice question is an incomplete sentence or question which has several answers from which one is to be chosen.

Example

Which of the following would help to win over a new customer?

a. Emphasizing the benefits of the product to the customer.

b. Being aggressive and pushy with the customer.

c. Selling only on price.

d. Not taking account of the customer's needs.

Matching lists: this compares one list of questions with a second list of possible answers. The aim is to match each of the answers on the second list to one question in the first list.

Example

Technical risk	Customer needs to be certain that price corresponds to value.
Financial risk	A product typifies a certain socio-economic group in society.
Physical risk	The customer is afraid the product may not work reliably.
Psychological risk	The customer sees a danger of injury.
Social risk	The customer wants a product to match his/her own self-image.

True-false statements: the object of this test is for the trainee to determine whether each statement is true or false, or requires a yes or no answer.

Example

True	False	
----	----	1. Exercise and diet have nothing to do with a positive attitude.
----	----	2. A positive attitude is not possible in all situations.
----	----	3. Daily exercise has a great impact on well-being at work.
----	----	4. The better you feel physically, the better you feel mentally.

Open questions: sometimes known as brief essay questions, open questions are a list of questions which begin with the words: who, what, why, where, when, which and how. These questions require an answer or explanation from the trainee – not just a yes or no.

Example

At the end of a course on customer care the following questions would require thought and analysis on the part of the trainee:
1. Why do your counter staff treat regular customers too routinely or too casually?
2. How much business have you lost in this financial year by customers deserting you?
3. What will you do about this lost business?
4. Which steps can you take to ensure regular customers stay with you?

Oral tests: these are used to test knowledge or skills prior to training, and as a review and assessment of the acquired learning at the end of training. An oral test is often used in conjunction with a performance test.

Pilot tests: whatever method of testing is chosen, trainees may react in a wide variety of ways, ranging from rejection of the test to being completely intimidated.

For this reason you may need a pilot test – a small sample test used on a selected number of trainees to assess and evaluate learning. Tests which produce the most consistent results are then used on a wider scale.

Post-course questionnaire

This questionnaire is different from the trainee's end of course questionnaire which is completed by the trainee at the end of a training session.

The post-course questionnaire can be completed either by the trainer after completion of a training course, or by the line manager in a debriefing session. Principal questions are:

- What training needs have been satisfied?
- What factors prevented the trainee from learning?
- How suitable were the trainer's methods and procedures?

- What changes would you suggest to improve the course?
- Which subjects were most beneficial?
- Which topics were least relevant or beneficial?

- What additional learning took place that was not intended or expected?
- What changes in job performance can be expected as a result of the training programme?
- What specific action will be taken as a result of the course?

Follow-up interview

The interview is a very effective method of evaluating learning at the end of a training session. As a two-way exchange of information, it has the advantage of being structured formally or informally. The interview can help determine behavioural changes, and assess specific knowledge or skills acquired through training. The trainee's personality, as well as what was understood of the training experience, comes across in an interview.

The interviewer must be well prepared and have drafted a list of topics in advance. In order to plan, direct and control the interview, an interviewer should know what to look for, and how to find it. An interview should last approximately 20–40 minutes. These are the points to consider for the interview:

- The training objectives
- The course content and methodology
- Know what information is required
- Be a good listener
- Ask open questions
- Give positive and constructive feedback
- Establish a mutually agreed action plan

Trainer's Tip
The ability to ask good questions and listen intelligently are two key skills to be developed by all trainers.

Example – The Interview

Name of Trainee: Date of Course:
Job Title: Date of Interview:
Course Attended:
Topics to be covered: Comments:

1. Were the training objectives achieved?
2. Which knowledge or skills tests were taken?
3. What is the trainee's impression of the course structure and content?
4. How does the trainee perceive the trainer?
5. What is the trainee's action plan?
6. How will training improve job performance?
7. How can training be applied most effectively?
8. What is the next step?

The interviewer should use a systematic method to record information during the interview, and to analyse the data at the end of the interview.

Direct on-job observation

Observing the trainee in the work place is an effective way to evaluate post-training performance. It can be used successfully in conjunction with an interview to improve the quality of information gathered. On-job observation has the advantage of:

- Gaining a clear picture of the trainee in the work environment
- Not interfering with daily work
- Working flexibly with the trainee

Observation can help to gain an understanding of employee job responsibilities, and is a way to determine which training will most benefit the trainee. An agreed period of time should be dedicated to observing the trainee perform specific tasks on the job.

On the other hand, disadvantages to this particular method are that the job holder may:

- Feel intimidated at such close scrutiny
- Feel that the reason for on-job observation is due to personal inadequacy
- Misunderstand and feel that his/her job is threatened
- Feel the observer is not properly qualified to understand this particular job role

A supervised special project

The supervised special project is another method of evaluating on-job performance and behaviour. A trainer or manager assigns a project to be completed by a set date, and analyses how well the trainee plans, organizes and manages the project.

The project should be continually monitored to ensure that the trainee is proceeding according to the agreed budget and plan. The trainee should report to a line manager on progress at regular intervals.

The value of a supervised special project is that it emphasizes the role of planning, extends knowledge and develops skills. Another advantage is that managing a project tends to exact a change in attitude, particularly if completion of the project demands assistance from colleagues or other departments.

Managing a project provides a new experience and an opportunity to extend knowledge over a wider range of problems than normally experienced on the job, and to exercise analytical skills in solving problems related to the job or work environment.

A regular performance appraisal

The appraisal system is a formal process which measures current levels of performance, comparing them to past levels of performance. The process of studying employee performance is to determine what impact individual performance has on organizational performance and profit.

It is essential, in any organization, that the performance appraisal process is formally linked to training. This is because the appraisal system provides the means to accomplish these tasks:

- To identify training needs prior to training
- To appraise whether training has been applied in the workplace
- To assess what impact improved performance has on profit

Like the testing method, the performance appraisal process acts as a guide – a guide to selection of the right training for an individual, and to ascertain how successful specific training has been both for the individual and the organization. Chapter 18 examines the performance appraisal process.

Responsibility for Monitoring and Reporting

The best person to monitor the effect of training on the individual and the department is the line manager in close liaison with the training manager.

Although every department will be responsible for communicating the results of training, it will be the task of the head of training to collate, analyse and organise this information in a final report for presentation and evaluation at the end of the year.

Compilation of the results of training

Compilation of regular reports to analyse overall employee performance is an important aspect of measuring results. The ideal way to compile your report depends on the reason for reporting, ie the need for a discussion document, a regular review meeting, or the end of year assessment. There are four basic types of report:

The persuasive report: this presents an assessment of the training situation and recommends a specific course of action. This may refer to an individual, a group, a department or the organization overall as a result of the year's training

The persuasive report analyses the problem, evaluates possible solutions, and recommends a course of action through persuasive arguments which relate training benefits to the individual and the organization.

The informative report: this type of report is usually a brief, unbiased summary of the training situation; its purpose is to educate the reader about the background or history of a training predicament or circumstance.

An informative report may be used to explain the history of training in the organization, the training programmes used in the past by a particular department, or explain the current and past thinking of the training department prior to an annual review.

The explanatory report: this type of report is excellent for setting out a great amount of detail. It can be used to examine a particular aspect of training which requires attention.

For example, this may be the planned expenditure for the year, an evaluation of costs and performance during the last financial year, or a review and analysis of training programmes and the number of employees trained throughout the year.

The discussive report: this should be prepared prior to a discussion, departmental meeting or brainstorming session. This type of report is not meant to suggest action, it only outlines topics for discussion, consideration or negotiation.

For example, a discussive report may highlight the reasons for expanding the training department, recruiting new trainers or appointing an outside consultant.

Conclusion

In this chapter we have examined how to monitor and report the results of training. The main topics surveyed are:

- Evaluation of training objectives and whether they have been achieved
- How effective the transfer of learning has been to the work environment
- The various methods that can be used to reflect the success of training
- Whose responsibility it is to report the results of training within the organization

▶ **CHAPTER REVIEW** ◀

1. Measuring and proving results of training effectiveness can be accomplished successfully by:
   - Evaluating training objectives
   - Assessing the transfer of learning
   - Choosing the appropriate method of evaluation
2. To appraise whether training objectives are met requires several different methods to which the trainer, line manager and trainee are committed:
   - pre-course briefing
   - the training contract
   - end of course evaluation
   - post-course debriefing
   - post-training audit
   - performance appraisal
3. There are a wide variety of methods to choose from to execute the post-training audit. They include:
   - trainee action plan
   - testing
   - post-course questionnaire
   - follow-up interview
   - direct on-job observation
   - supervised special project
   - regular performance appraisal
4. It is ultimately the responsibility of the head of training to monitor and report the results of training within the organization.
5. There are four basic types of report to compile the results of training:
   - Persuasive
   - Informative
   - Explanatory
   - Discussive

14 Selecting an External Training Consultant

▷   CHAPTER SUMMARY   ◁

When and how to recruit external training consultants.
- Why recruit an external consultant?
- Types of external training courses
- The selection process
- Word-of-mouth recommendations

Why Recruit an External Consultant?

An organization which perceives training as an ingredient for success may at some time augment its own training resources with those of an external consultancy.

External trainers can often be used where your internal training team lacks manpower, expertise, experience, time or credibility. A small organization may not have the resources to employ its own team of internal trainers. The following are several circumstances which indicate a need for an external consultant:

- Your trainers do not have the expertise to deliver training on a specific subject
- Your internal training capabilities have been temporarily stretched to their limit
- An external consultancy has been asked to undertake a work-study programme, and the training function is included in this programme

- Management seeks reassurance that its decisions are valid, and an external consultant offers a different and more objective point of view
- The organization needs to augment its training resources (eg absentee staff, to maintain a budget limit)

A range of advantages makes the use of an external consultant viable:

- Expertise in a wider range of subjects than is available in-house
- The provision of a range of training facilities to which you do not have access in-house
- Introduction and exchange of new ideas with external trainers who deal with a wide range of organizations
- The opportunity for trainers to participate in courses where they can exchange ideas and problems with colleagues in other departments or trainers in other market sectors

The factors which determine whether the use of an external consultant is really necessary are:

- The types of external training courses you require
- The selection process
- Word-of-mouth recommendations

Types of External Training Courses

Having determined which knowledge or skills are lacking within your training team, what type of training courses are available? Three possibilities present themselves:

1. A tailor-made programme to suit your organizational needs
2. An existing public course for individual employees to attend
3. A course which offers a specific recognized qualification.

Tailor-made training programmes

An external consultant can produce and deliver a new training programme designed specifically for the needs of your organization.

Example

A leading insurance organization with its own team of professional in-house trainers recently commissioned a training course for their tele-sales staff. The in-company trainers were looking for new ideas and a fresh approach to complement the tele-sales training sessions they had delivered in the past two years.

A training consultancy was chosen to produce and deliver the new training; a selected number of staff in the organization's south-eastern branches underwent training with the external consultancy.

Two in-house trainers from the insurance company sat in on the new training programmes. This was with a view to taking over future training of all UK tele-sales staff – to save on costs.

It was agreed with the consultancy that the programme and the tailor-made training notes would be adopted in the following months by the internal team of trainers. The two trainers who had attended the training sessions were responsible for training the in-house trainers to deliver the new programme.

The tele-sales staff in the south-east branches increased their sales substantially. A national drive to deliver the new tele-sales programmes was implemented by the internal training team to all remaining tele-sales staff nation-wide.

Open, public courses

External training consultancies offer open course programmes. An open programme is a public course which is attended by trainees from several different organizations and is held at an outside venue.

This is quite common when the identification of training needs (for the organization and the individual) shows that training is required for a specific subject which is not included in your training prospectus, or your trainers are not considered to have the relevant experience to offer a particular course.

Example

A national restaurant chain became aware of the newly-publicized dangers relating to the handling and storage of dairy products. They sent their catering staff on a series of open courses to learn new methods of hygiene and refrigeration related to dairy produce.

Qualification training

Some training organizations offer long-term courses which are approved by various institutions relevant to specific fields in the private and public sector. There are university or polytechnic degree courses, diplomas such as the City and Guilds, the Business and Technician Education Council (BTEC), and the CNAA (Council for National Academic Awards).

To satisfy an immediate training need, you may prefer a short course which is validated with the National Council for Vocational Qualifications (NCVQ). The NCVQ liaise with employers and examining bodies to provide vocational qualifications which are accepted at a national level.

> **Trainer's Tip**
>
> NVQs (national vocational qualifications) are statements of competence in specific fields, and have been introduced in many industrial and commercial sectors; for example, agriculture, hotel and catering, engineering and computer technology. To qualify for a certificate in a particular area, credits or units of competence must be accrued.
>
> The NCVQ is purely an accrediting body and does not issue certificates of qualification. The NCVQ publishes the criteria for national vocational qualifications.
>
> The awarding bodies are institutes such as the RSA, the City and Guilds, and the Institute of Training and Development (ITD). For more information consult Shirley Fletcher's book, *NVQs, Standards and Competence* (1991).
>
> American national standards are set by the International Association for Continuing Education and Training, in Washington D.C. This organization sets and promotes generic CEU's (continuing education units) for training and education in all fields. It is not a regulatory body.

Due to time restraints, a short external course may be preferred to satisfy quickly a specific training need within the organization. When interviewing a designated number of training consultants, ask which of their courses are accredited by an institution or government scheme which is pertinent to your organizational sector.

Example
A large construction company wished to apply for British Standard 5750 (BS5750). To win the seal of approval, the organization was asked to retrain its current team of electrical engineers.

The internal training team was not able to offer the course in electrical engineering which was needed to bring the team up to the required national quality standards.

The regional training board was consulted, and the team was sent on an external open course which offered the necessary certification.

What courses or subjects do you require?

The range of skills and talents varies with each trainer on your team. To select which external training courses or subjects are necessary to buy in, you should:

- Identify employee training needs
- Define training objectives
- Identify which training objectives cannot be met in-house
- List the range of subjects by priority
- Note how many employees need similar training
- Decide which external courses are required

The Selection Process

Once you have decided to approach an external trainer or consultant, it is important to:

- Draw up a comprehensive list of potential suppliers
- Interview a selected number and draw up a shortlist
- Evaluate their proposals and determine who will win the contract
- Brief your final candidate

There are a multitude of professional bodies and independent training institutes who offer advice on training in all sectors of commerce, industry and the arts. Among these are your local government training boards, appropriate trade and industry associations, local training and enterprise councils, and local manpower networks.

Seven main organizations involved in training and development in the UK have formed a partnership called the Human Resource

Development Partnership (HRDP). Their aims are to promote the government's business growth training scheme, to support Training and Enterprise Councils (TECs) and the National Training Task Force. The organizations are:

- Institute of Personnel Management (IPM)
- Institute of Training and Development (ITD)
- British Institute of Management (BIM)
- British Association for Commercial and Industrial Education (BACIE)
- National Economic Development Office (NEDO)
- Department of Employment (ED)
- The Industrial Society (IS)

Trainer's Tip

Many industrial and commercial sectors are covered by independent or voluntary training organizations.

For advice consult the Institute of Personnel Management, the Industrial Training Board, or the British Institute of Management. You may wish to refer to the current (annual) *Training Directory* (ITD, BACIE and Kogan Page).

The ASTD (American Society for Training and Development) is the American professional association for trainers. The society's head office is based in Alexandria, Virginia, with local chapters in individual states. Information on suppliers of training is provided in the ASTD *Buyer's Guide*.

How comprehensive and updated is your file of training consultants?

Prior to selecting the external organization which is relevant to your needs, draw up a comprehensive list of consultants. As this is a time-consuming task, it would be wise to continually update your sources of information, keeping up-to-date brochures, advertisements and any promotional material on file.

Trainer's Tip

Approach external consultancies with care. Many training consultancies provide a premium service, but there are others whose competence and success is questionable.

- Choose a reputable firm
- Interview and brief the senior consultants and the relevant trainers

137

- Clarify all costs
- Evaluate costs and value for money
- Attend a sample training session before making your final decision
- Be available on the day to introduce trainees to the new consultants

The following are useful sources of information:

Mail-shots, advertising and sales promotion material: during the course of a financial year, many training bodies and organizations mail shot organizations who are likely to be interested in their training courses. There are thousands of consultants who provide training, and they will not all have written to you!

It is important to keep on file those training brochures which are relevant to your field, and to keep track of relevant advertisements you see from time to time in the trade and consumer press. Also appropriate may be sales promotion leaflets inserted into trade or consumer journals. These leaflets, specific to a training organization, contain information on tailor-made and open course programmes.

Industrial training organizations (ITOs): there are well over 100 independent training organizations which operate in various industrial sectors. They often do not have any legislative authority.

Your industrial training organization (or its registered voluntary counterpart) can provide a service and offer practical help. Your local further education institution may also proffer advice. Many colleges and universities now extend training to commerce and industry.

National Training Index (NTI): subscribers to the Index obtain information on training organizations and their services, as well as references from individuals who have attended courses. The NTI offers comprehensive information and advice on business training courses, computer-based training and open learning packages.

National training and consultancy providers: Many directories list established national training providers; they are often available on subscription or from the business section of your local bookshop. Keep an eye out for those approved providers whose programmes are accredited training schemes.

Due to government and European Community (EC) interest in developing the future of training and development, it is becoming more important for national training providers to be accredited for their training programmes. In the future, it will be possible for those delegates who have attended training programmes with an external consultant to build up a string of credits. These credits can be applied to a diploma or certificate in the appropriate field of expertise.

TECs and LECs: the Training and Enterprise Councils of England and Wales, and the Local Enterprise Companies of Scotland are principal advisers in the national training framework.

They reflect national and local government-led training initiatives, and receive significant grants and programme funding. The annual *Training Directory* lists the national TECs and LECs.

National Training Task Force (NTTF): this was set up to cover national training issues, and is responsible for commissioning research and investigating employer investment in training. The NTTF reports to the government Secretary for Employment.

Word-of-mouth Recommendations

Never underestimate the potential of your network of contacts. They are an invaluable source of information. Trusted colleagues and contacts can offer opinions on external training consultants within your field.

Do, however, approach these word-of-mouth recommendations with some caution. A training consultancy which has worked well for another organization may not be quite as successful with yours. It is important to consider:

- The external consultancy's particular experience in your field
- Whether you can develop a rapport with the external trainers
- The experience and suitability of their trainers
- How costs fit into your budget

Conclusion

There are a variety of reasons why organizations choose to augment their own training resources with those of an external training consultant or supplier.

Before selecting an external provider of training, it is important to analyse which skills or training programmes are lacking within your organization, and to determine which training programmes should be bought in.

► **CHAPTER REVIEW** ◄

1. External training providers or suppliers are often recruited to train in areas where internal trainers lack manpower, experience, expertise, time or credibility.

2. There are three types of external training courses:
   1. Tailor-made training programmes
   2. Open, public courses
   3. Qualification training

3. To select appropriate external training it is important to:
   - Identify employee training needs
   - Define training objectives
   - Identify which training objectives cannot be met in-house
   - List the range of subjects by priority
   - Note how many employees need similar training
   - Decide which external courses are required

4. To approach an external consultancy:
   - Draw up a comprehensive list of potential suppliers
   - Interview a selected number and draw up a shortlist
   - Evaluate their proposals and determine who will win the contract
   - Brief your final candidate

15 Preparing Your Brief for an External Consultancy

▷   CHAPTER SUMMARY   ◁

Careful briefing of your short-listed training providers and a thorough evaluation of their presentations and training proposals are significant factors in the final selection of an external training organization. This chapter examines the:
- Preparation of your brief
- Evaluation of the consultant's presentation
- What to look for in a proposal
- Final discussions

Preparation of your Brief

An external training consultant can often offer excellent resources and top training talent to a training programme.

External consultants have a wider range of knowledge about all aspects of the training business than any one single client company may have. Training consultancies depend on competition, and each provider is anxious to outperform its rivals.

It is important to consider what information you wish to give the consultant, and what further research you will request them to do for you.

You need to consider what supporting material may be useful to their understanding of your organizational training needs. For example:

- History and background of your organization
- Product and service information
- Corporate mission and culture
- Current in-house training programmes
- Profile of internal trainers
- Your organization's training methods, style and strategy

As an outline to help you produce your brief, the following topics should be considered:

- What is the objective of buying in training?
- Who is the training aimed at?
- How many people require training?

- What is the subject matter of the training?
- What is the projected timing of the training?
- How much money is available?

- What is the type of training required?
- How many external trainers are needed?
- Will your trainers be involved in the process?

Is your brief concise yet comprehensive?

You may decide to ask half a dozen training consultants to present their credentials. This may include an explanation of their existing client programmes, with no discussion of what they might do for your business at this point. The advantage of this strategy is that you avoid giving an outside supplier confidential company information. It also gives you time to select a short list of potential candidates.

You may choose to present your detailed brief to a short-list of two or three suppliers. Your brief must include an analysis of your organization, its training mission, objectives and policies.

Trainer's Tip
For reasons of security, you may choose to brief only one organization in detail.

The following three-step programme protects classified or restricted information in your organization or market sector. This applies to many firms whose business is involved in new research and technology, the defence industry, or a highly competitive environment.

Step One
Dependent on your line of business, if it is imperative that all information imparted to an outside organization remains confidential, you may prefer to outline only basic details about your training needs when interviewing and briefing potential external trainers.

Therefore, you may choose to interview several training organizations, having briefed them on your training objectives only. It is at that point you can compile your short-list.

Step Two
Upon receipt of basic training proposals from the short-listed candidates, you are in a position to make your final choice. Examine the proposals carefully and query any details which are not clear or contradict any points raised during the interview.

Step Three
The final step is to present your detailed brief to the one final candidate who will then propose a more detailed programme according to your specific training needs.

Evaluation of the Consultant's Presentation

When selecting and recruiting an outside training organization, consider the quality and professionalism of their presentation.

To determine whether their organization will be compatible with yours, it is important to draw up a list of criteria you are looking for from their presentation. See Chapter 16 for a more comprehensive look at criteria for selecting an external training consultancy.

Trainer's Tip
There are two basic ingredients to a successful and persuasive presentation, ie the verbal and non-verbal messages.

Verbal communication
Verbal information is achieved via the message and the voice – the meaning and content of the words chosen, and the timbre, tone and attitude which is portrayed.

Non-verbal communication
Non-verbal information is portrayed through body language –

gestures and congruence: whether the words match the gestures. Does the speaker's presence communicate sincerity, enthusiasm and energy?

CHECKLIST
Useful for formal or informal presentations.
1. How effectively did they communicate their message?
2. How skilled were they in making a prepared presentation?
3. How many trainers were involved in the presentation?
4. Did they use visual aids in their presentation?
5. How did they enhance their presentation?
6. How long was their presentation?
7. How effectively did they involve you?
8. How well did they use their voices?
9. What was their body language saying?
10. Were they comfortable, relaxed and persuasive?
11. How well did they deal with your questions?
12. Were they able to motivate you with their enthusiasm?
13. How interested are they in your business?
14. What information do they require from you to prepare a proposal?
15. Do you feel you can work with them?
16. Why or why not?

Trainer's Tip – Visual Aids
It is important to analyse the use of visual aids in a presentation as it will give an indication of the quality of visual aids used during their training sessions.
A formal presentation may include such items as:
- 35 mm slides
- Overhead acetates
- Desktop presenters
- Video tapes or films
- Computer-generated graphics
- Selected pieces of equipment
- Demonstration of techniques or procedures
- Flip charts or whiteboards

If you are satisfied with the presentation, ask the training consultancy to send you a written proposal.

What to look for in a Proposal

Proposals are an important part of tendering for your business. They have a major impact on your final decision. If an external training consultancy is writing a proposal designed to gain your business, you should examine the layout and content of the proposal in detail. Points to consider are the:

Introduction: to explain the objectives of the proposal.

Summary of contents: an outline of the proposal. This is a brief overview of their ultimate recommendations. These may be presented in bullet point format.

The current situation: what they understand of your organization, your training philosophy and current training objectives. This part of the proposal should show intelligence and imagination.

Courses of action: what action do they suggest?

Full recommendations: these should be based on all the facts. Included should be:

- The training objectives
- Recommended courses
- An outline of all course programmes
- Who is responsible for the design and production of course materials
- Costs and fee structure

Conclusions: these show the benefits of the recommendations. For example, cost savings, increased performance, improved knowledge or skills, enhanced customer relations, etc.

Terms of business:

- Their business policy (eg to run quality courses with small numbers for maximum training effectiveness)
- Their published fee structure and all extra costs
- Their terms and method of payment

Final Discussions

Many factors will influence your choice of consultant, including their style and presentation. Eventually, having taken into account training experience, reputation, costs and the training consultant's written proposal, you will be in a position to make your final decision.

Having made your decision and selected a training consultant to design and deliver your new training programme, you will need to

clarify the following points before implementing their training programmes:

1. Have you briefed the external trainers thoroughly on your
   organization's training objectives and training policies?
2. Carefully examine the proposed outline of their training
   programmes.
3. Read and edit their suggested training notes or materials to
   ensure they are appropriate to your needs.
4. Clarify all fees and the terms and method of payment.
5. Arrange to deal directly with the trainers responsible for all
   training activity – this includes designers and deliverers of
   training.

Conclusion

Carefully consider the information to be presented to training consultants, and design a concise yet comprehensive brief which will
outline your training objectives and reasons for choosing an external
consultant.

To make your final decision, carefully analyse the presentations
made to you. Finally, evaluate their training proposals to determine
which consultant is best suited to your organization's needs and
policies.

▶   **CHAPTER REVIEW**   ◀

1. Preparation of a brief to present to potential training suppliers is an important element in the selection process.
2. A brief should include the following topics:
   - What is the objective?
   - Who is the training aimed at?
   - How many people require training?
   - What is the training subject matter?
   - What is the projected timing?

   - How much money is available?
   - What type of training is required?
   - How many external trainers do you need?
   - Will your trainers be involved?
3. Carefully evaluate the presentations made by candidates, and draw up a checklist of key points to consider.
4. A proposal is an important aspect in your choice of training consultant. Points to consider are the:
   - introduction
   - summary of contents
   - current situation
   - courses of action
   - full recommendations
   - conclusions
   - terms of business
5. A final discussion or meeting prior to implementing the training is essential.
   - Fully brief all the trainers
   - Examine their proposal in detail
   - Read and edit all training notes and materials
   - Clarify fees and costs
   - Deal directly with the trainers

16 Criteria for Selecting an External Trainer

▷   CHAPTER SUMMARY   ◁

Which skills, experience and background do you require from an external
training consultant? In order to determine this, you will need to draw up a list of
criteria with which to evaluate the presentations and training proposals made by
external training consultants.
- Checklist of criteria
- Cost-benefit analysis
- Final survey
- Reporting your decision

Checklist of Criteria

The criteria against which you should evaluate your final decision
encompass many different areas. Some of the factors to be examined
are:

- The background of the consultancy
- Their training experience in your field and in general
- How their organization is structured
- The professionalism of their presentation
- The validity and relevance of their proposal

Activity

1. Brainstorming

   With the colleagues who will help you to select an external training consultant, devise a list of the major criteria you expect from him or her. Do not worry at the size of the list – in a brainstorming session the idea is to generate as many ideas as possible.

2. Master List

   Categorize your list. Place the criteria in order of priority. Eliminate the items which are not relevant or of immediate importance.

Your master list may look similar to the one below:

General background

- How long have they been in the training business?
- What services do they offer?
- How many accounts do they have?
- What is their percentage of open courses vs tailor-made courses?
- What subjects or fields do they specialize in?
- How do these compare with your organizational needs?

General Attitude

- What kind of people work within the consultancy?
- Are they keen to work with you?
- Which type of training are they most experienced in (ie tailor-made or open, public courses)?

Compatibility

- How well did they understand and interpret your brief?
- What is the likelihood of building a good rapport and a working relationship with their trainers?
- How compatible is their senior management with you and your team?

Experience

- Do they have experience in your sector?
- What similar client accounts have they handled?
- How important is it that they understand your market, industrial or economic sector?
- How do they approach problems?

- Is their approach intelligent and logical?
- How different is their approach to problems compared to yours?
- What experience can they offer which your team of trainers lacks?
- How much experience do they have in consultancy and problem solving?

Organization

- What is the structure of their training consultancy?
- Are they well organized?
- How long have they been operating in this manner?
- Are they prepared to work in all areas of your business?

Perceived Ability

- How did you hear about them?
- What is their reputation and image in the training field?
- What is their share of the training market place?
- Are they considered to be innovative or tried and true?
- What is the method, style and strategy of their training?
- Do their trainers have flair and personality?

Costs

- How do their costs compare to the other suppliers on your short list?
- How do their costs compare to their perceived value?
- What are their costs per day and per trainee?
- How do these costs fit into your budget?
- Is it more cost effective to run an in-company session or to send your trainees on an open course?
- What would be the method of payment?

Cost-benefit Analysis

Like any other business, costs are the deciding factor in whether you use an external training consultant. There are many ways to cut costs. Beware of cutting too many corners and therefore impairing the quality of the desired training. You may reduce costs in a number of ways:

- Offer the services of your training administrators

- Authorize the outside consultant to use your office machines and equipment
- Produce and provide any course materials and equipment that are required
- Use your own premises for the training programmes

> **Trainer's Tip**
> *Financial constraints*
> Training strategies have to be balanced against financial constraints. In the event of employing an outside training consultant, your budget plays a deciding factor.
>
> Training objectives must be confirmed with all those involved (management and trainees) before any interviews with external consultants are conducted and/or training programmes undertaken.
> *Training costs*
> Training costs may be evaluated in relation to value added, or as a proportion of, total personnel costs.
> *Benefits*
> What is the benefit of employing this particular external consultant compared with the cost of recruiting and implementing their programmes?
>
> Benefits may be increased productivity, enhanced performance or morale, improved attitude to the job.

Final Survey

Have you considered all the important aspects of hiring an external training consultant?

What will the external trainer provide?

You will need to confirm with the training consultancy what they will be responsible for in terms of consultancy days, production and delivery of training programmes, schedules, timing and training administration.

Consultancy days: the outside agency may need to spend a certain amount of time within the organization. This may include interviewing staff to be trained, learning how the organization works on a daily basis, coming to terms with problems and how they may be resolved.

If consultancy time is required, list the objectives, the tasks and the

151

costs involved. This will help to decide how many consultancy days will be required, what the objectives are, and how the costs fit into your budget.

Objectives may include a calculation of training programmes, to whom the training should be delivered, over what period of time, and whether tailor-made or public courses are suitable.

Production and delivery of training programmes: it is important to ascertain who will be responsible for the design and delivery of the new training programmes. Very often with outside training consultants, one consultant evaluates the situation and another delivers the training.

Some training consultancies delegate a training consultant to produce an overview of what training will be required within an organization. At that point, the same consultant may:

- Design the material personally and ask another trainer to deliver the training
- Delegate the design and production of a training programme to another trainer who subsequently delivers the training

This can affect whether the trainer understands your organization and your training objectives. You do not want a new trainer, whom you have never met, to show up to deliver training on the designated day.

Schedules and timing: the timing of external training programmes is an essential element of your final selection. Ensure that you have discussed the availability of trainers and consultants for any tailor-made training. If you plan to send trainees on an open programme, ensure that course places are available on dates which suit your needs.

When recruiting staff from the workplace, consideration must be made for holidays, and the availability of substitute personnel to compensate for those absent.

Training administration: before signing a contract with an external training consultant, it is important to determine who will handle all the training administration. This takes into account who will be responsible for booking and organizing the necessary training venues, and who will design and produce all of the necessary training materials.

What equipment will you be expected to provide as the client for a tailor-made course, and what equipment will the trainer bring to the training programmes? It is not unusual for a training organization to prefer to use their own equipment. This reduces the risk of failure and ensures they deliver training programmes to a certain standard.

Whose responsibility will it be to provide course notes and materials? It may possible to reduce costs if the training department in your organization agrees to provide files, pens and photo-copied notes on the day. This means the external trainer only needs to provide a disc or hard copy of the training notes for your administrators.

The checklist provides a useful final survey.

CHECKLIST

1. Check consultants' references and reputation with previous users.
2. Compare their advertising and sales promotion activities with other external training consultancies. What does the quality of their campaign tell you about the quality of their work?
3. Double check that they qualify in any areas of special expertise you need (eg EC harmonization, legal or financial requirements).
4. Who is responsible for briefing line management and trainees on the external training?
5. Have you met all the trainers who will be delivering training within your organization, and discussed their background, credentials and expertise?
6. Will the external trainer provide all course notes and materials?
7. Who will book and organize an external training venue if required?
8. What equipment will you be expected to provide?
9. What equipment will the external trainer supply?
10. What post-training feedback do you want from your external training consultant?
11. How well does the fee structure compare with the quality and amount of activity to be undertaken?
12. How does their fee compare in the market-place? Does it represent value for money?

Reporting your Decision

Once you have established the general background and experience of the consultancy and its trainers, examined their experience in training, identified their compatibility with your team of trainers, determined how well they understand your organization and market sector, and examined the costs involved – you are ready to report your findings to management. The following points provide an outline for your report:

Writing your report

1. What skills, experience and background do you expect from an external training consultant?
2. What can your final candidate offer that your team of trainers cannot provide in-house?
3. How do their trainers compare with your team in terms of professionalism, expertise and credibility?
4. Who are their current clients?
5. Are any of these clients competitors?
6. Can your trainers sit in and observe a training session prior to signing a contract?
7. Can your trainers observe the new training sessions to be implemented for the organization?
8. Once a tailor-made course has been designed, can you have use of the materials to run your own in-company sessions?
9. What is the comparison of costs versus the benefits of external training?
10. How will the training be validated and evaluated?

Another advantage of using external training consultants is that an independent and dispassionate point of view is obtained. They can work without the influence of internal pressures and constraints that an internal team of trainers deals with on a daily basis.

To implement new suggestions or programmes successfully, it is essential to involve personnel from within the organization. Be wary of a consultant who makes grandiose suggestions which do not take account of the organization's existing or available resources.

Conclusion

The compilation of a list of criteria can assist in selecting the external training consultant. A brainstorming session is the ideal way to draw up a list.

A cost-benefit analysis will help to evaluate the benefits of external training compared to the costs involved.

► **CHAPTER REVIEW** ◄

1. A checklist of criteria to select an external training consultant includes:
   - background of the organization
   - training experience
   - structure of the organization
   - professionalism of their presentation
   - validity of their training proposal
2. Your master list of criteria should incorporate these categories:
   - general background
   - general attitude
   - compatibility
   - experience
   - organization
   - perceived training
   - ability
   - costs
3. A cost-benefit analysis is necessary to evaluate the benefits of employing an external training consultant compared to the costs incurred.
4. A final checklist when hiring an external supplier of training considers:
   - what the external trainer will provide
   - required consultancy days and their cost
   - production and delivery of training programmes
   - schedules and timing
   - training administration
   - feedback
5. Your report to management on your choice of external training consultant should outline: their general background and experience in training, their general understanding of your organization and market sector, and the costs involved.

17 Advantages and Disadvantages of External Courses

▷   **CHAPTER SUMMARY**   ◁

You have three choices of external training programmes. This chapter studies their advantages and disadvantages:
1. Open, public courses
2. Tailor-made training
3. Open courses held in-company

Open, Public Courses

These are training courses which have been previously designed by an external training consultancy, and are used on pre-specified dates – either at a public venue such as a hotel, or at the training consultant's own training site. Trainees attend from many different locations and organizations.

Public courses range from the small participative workshop of two or more trainees, to a large seminar or lecture attended by several hundred trainees.

Most external training consultancies produce a leaflet or brochure several times a year with programme details, timings and costs. As direct marketing has become one of the fastest growing methods of promoting training, many organizations target a specific audience to mail-shot with leaflets, brochures and incentives to attend their open courses.

Reasons for choosing open, public courses

- Only a few individuals require training
- Several employees require individual and separate training
- Costs can be spread across a longer accounting period

If several employees require training in the same field, but they need to be trained separately, then it is a great advantage to select an open, public course which each employee can attend individually. This is sometimes dictated by the need to boost confidence or improve motivation. The training can be booked for separate dates, and the costs spread across a greater time span.

Example

Recently, a firm experienced a particular problem with two senior secretaries.

They had created such a personality conflict between themselves that the entire staff had become involved. One of the main reasons for this was the inability of the responsible line manager to deal with the problem from the beginning. The staff felt they were being coerced into choosing sides. The atmosphere was deteriorating markedly in this small family firm of only 30 employees.

It was suggested that both employees attend two separate training courses. One was sent on a customer care course which concentrated on improving relations with colleagues and customers. The other secretary was sent on an assertiveness course to help her realize the effect her aggressive behaviour had on others.

The specific objective for both secretaries was the same – to effect change in their behaviour on the job. It was a priority to improve the behaviour of the two secretaries in order to repair the damage done to company morale. It was decided that if the training had the desired results, other staff would be trained in the appropriate areas to avoid future problems.

The external trainer was well-briefed, and the post-training briefing sessions concentrated on behavioural action plans to help the two secretaries work together more effectively.

Advantages of open, public courses

- It may be more cost effective to send one, or a small number of trainees, on a course which requires distance travelling and time off-site.
- The cost of training employees on an individual or small numbers basis can ensure that the cost of training is spread over a longer period of time.
- Training employees on open, public courses offers them an opportunity to share problems and ideas with delegates in other industries and economic sectors.
- An open, public course offers thinking and planning time away from the work environment.
- Sending an individual on an open, public course can provide motivation that on-site training would not offer.

  This is because the employee will feel that s/he has been chosen specifically to pilot the training, to test a particular training course, or that the company feels s/he is worth investing in.

Example

An international pharmaceutical organization invested money over three years sending various staff on selected training programmes designed and delivered at public venues around the country.

The benefits to the company were that the cost of training had been spread across a long period of time, and the trainees had been trained as and when the need arose. It removed the employees from the working environment for only one day at a time.

The end result was increased motivation, and a feeling that the organization believed enough in them to finance special training on an individual basis. Job performance was enhanced as a result of the training.

Disadvantages of open, public courses

- Comparatively high cost of sending trainees
- Valuable time spent away from the workplace
- Possible inconsistency of training
- The course is not under the organization's control
- The course is not specific to your organization

Enrolling a number of employees on an external training course costs a lot. Costs typically include course fees, meals, accommodation and travel expenses. If this is the case, it may be more feasible to contemplate an in-company course delivered on your premises (or at a nearby site) by the external trainer.

The amount of time taken out of the workplace may be considerable. This is often the case if the open course lasts longer than one day. It is important to perform a cost-benefit analysis. This is to determine if the benefits of attending the external course outweigh the problems which arise when employees are absent from the workplace.

Employees attending different courses with various trainers will have differing experiences. An open, public course cannot be under the direct control of the organization, and the courses are not specific to your organization or sector.

Tailor-made Training

The majority of external training consultancies are pleased to negotiate in-house training directly with potential clients. Following a briefing session with a client, a training consultant or tutor will suggest a specific training programme or series of programmes.

It is your role, as client, to brief the external consultant as to your training priorities, objectives and needs. See Chapter 15 for a detailed appraisal of the training brief.

The consultant will make suggestions in the form of a proposal. The suggested programme will be specially designed to fit your organization and its training needs.

Reasons for choosing tailor-made training

- the training required is specific to your business
- a special kind of training is needed for a select number of employees
- the convenience and cost effectiveness
- to develop rapport and team spirit within the organization

Tailor-made training is necessary when your training needs are specific to your business and unlike any other sector, or a selected group of individuals within the organization have similar and simultaneous needs.

A course designed and delivered by an external trainer, on your

159

premises (or at a location convenient to you), is cost-effective. External training consultants will negotiate on price according to:

- the number of delegates to be trained
- the total number of training days required
- the amount of time needed to design and write training materials

Cost and convenience are the two usual criteria which affect the choice of location. You may prefer to train your staff off the premises at an outside venue, or to use a suitable room on-site.

Example
A small brokerage firm was interested in training its junior and senior managers in time management techniques. The company had spoken to several external training organizations and deduced that a one-day training session on their own premises would be the most effective use of time and money.

An external training consultant designed a programme specifically tailored to the needs of the firm. The course exercises complemented the daily work requirements of the junior and senior management team.

The entire management team was trained in the same skills on the same day, the training was cost effective, and a feeling of rapport and team spirit was developed between the two management teams.

Advantages of tailor-made training

- Training notes can be tailored to the specific needs of your organization
- Notes can be designed with your organization name and logo so that the notes are distinctive to your organization
- The training notes and exercises become the property of your organization and can be used again
- Course exercises and case studies can be designed for the size of groups you specify: pairs, small syndicate groups, larger groups
- Role-playing exercises can be designed with your individual products, services and employee needs in mind
- All the delegates attending the course will have common training objectives
- Tailor-made training offers an opportunity for employees

within an organization to work more closely with their colleagues from other departments
- Teamwork and shared problem solving is encouraged and can be transferred to the workplace
- The cost of sending all employees who need training on an open course may be prohibitive

Example

An industrial manufacturing firm requested a marketing course designed specifically for the industrial marketing sector. They wanted to train their brand managers in the general principles of marketing, but most general marketing courses concentrated on the retail sector.

Disadvantages of tailor-made training

The only reason may be that too few employees require training to make it cost-effective.

Open Courses held in-Company

It may suit your organization to commission an external training consultancy to give one of their open course programmes internally. This may be either on your premises or at a suitable local venue of your choosing.

Advantages of open courses held in-company

- The course notes have already been designed and produced
- Training can take place at a time convenient for you
- It is more cost-effective per trainee

As the course notes already exist, the only requirement is to select the venue, the trainees and a date. The employees can be trained immediately and concurrently, depending on the availability of the external trainer and venue.

Examples

1. A toy manufacturer based in the Midlands wanted to train its mobile sales team. It decided to use an external training consultancy

which had a perfect training course already designed. The sales team was based at branch offices around the country. A hotel near the head office in the Midlands was chosen for the training venue.

The hotel was chosen because it provided overnight accommodation and appropriate training facilities. There were no distractions, which allowed the sales representatives to concentrate on the two-day course.

It motivated them to work more closely together. There was a specific need to share problems and develop team rapport on the course as the sales representatives worked primarily alone in their sales regions.

2. A white goods manufacturer based in northwest London decided to use its own internal training facilities to train its receptionists in customer care. It bought an open course programme to be given by an external trainer. The reason for choosing an existing open course was primarily to save on costs.

However, a second reason for on-site training was to have access to the company showroom. This displayed a range of model kitchens and utility rooms with access to washing machines, dishwashers and microwaves. The showroom played an important part in the training.

Disadvantages of open courses held in-company

- The notes and exercises are not specific to your organization or market sector
- Some notes may need to be rewritten or redesigned

The real disadvantage of choosing an existing open programme to train your employees in-company, is that the course notes and exercises may not be targeted closely enough to your market sector.

Ask the trainer for an advance copy of the training notes and exercises for the open course. This way, you can decide if they are suitable.

It may be necessary to design, write, and add a small amount of material to cover the course and topics required.

Conclusion

There are three ways to train your employees when recruiting an external training organization.

They are: open, public courses which are held at a site selected by the external consultancy; tailor-made training courses designed specifically for your organization and held in-company; and open course programmes which are delivered internally.

▶ **CHAPTER REVIEW** ◀

1. In order to select which external training courses are the most suitable, compare your training needs against the advantages and disadvantages of each particular method.
2. An open, public course is designed by an external training organization. The training is delivered at a venue of their choice – usually a hotel or at their on-site training facilities.
3. The advantages of open courses are:
   - cost effective for a small number of trainees
   - to spread costs over a period of time
   - the opportunity to share problems with employees outside the organization
   - the opportunity to think and plan away from the daily work environment
   - an open course may be chosen for motivational reasons
4. Tailor-made training is designed by an external training consultancy to suit a client's specific training needs. The advantages of tailor-made training are:
   - training notes are tailored specifically to your organization and employee needs
   - notes can be distinctively produced with your organization's name and logo
   - you own the training notes
   - course exercises can be specifically designed for any size of group
   - role-playing exercises can be designed for your individual products, services and employees
   - the trainees will share common training objectives
   - an opportunity to work more closely with colleagues
   - teamwork and problem solving can be transferred to the workplace
   - costs of open course programmes may be prohibitive
5. Open courses held in-company can be adapted to a client's needs and delivered internally. Advantages of in-company open courses are:
   - course notes are already designed and written
   - training can take place immediately
   - it is more cost effective per trainee

18 The Performance Appraisal

▷	CHAPTER SUMMARY	◁

The performance appraisal is invaluable when formally reviewing job performance, and identifying training and development needs.
- What is a performance appraisal?
- The training link to the performance appraisal
- Who is responsible for co-ordinating appraisal data?

What is a Performance Appraisal?

A performance appraisal is a formal review of employee performance. At a performance appraisal, objectives or targets are agreed between manager and employee. At each subsequent appraisal, current and past performance is compared and targets are reviewed.

It is a prescribed system with a meeting arranged after a set period to review the targets set by the previous appraisal. This may be six-monthly or annually, depending on your organization.

None the less, the performance appraisal is not only a means to review performance standards and specific targets. It is a means to:

1. Identify current job performance levels
2. Identify individual employee strengths and weaknesses
3. Motivate and encourage the individual employee
4. Reward employees for their contribution to organizational objectives

5. Identify training and development needs
6. Identify potential performance standards
7. Plan future development of the individual
8. Discuss salary, promotion and training

The performance appraisal interview

At its simplest, the appraisal interview consists of three steps:

1. setting targets or standards
2. measuring performance
3. planning the appropriate action

A performance appraisal begins with an interview between manager and employee, an appraisal form is completed, and action is agreed. The action plan will specify targets to improve job performance, and indicate what is the reward for improvement. This reward may be a salary increase, job promotion, an opportunity to join a management development scheme, or to enrol in a new training programme.

Methods of reviewing performance

There are different methods of reviewing performance. The main types are: a management assessment of the employee, a grading system and a results-oriented approach. The most common method is results-oriented.

Management assessment of employee: the manager writes a brief report commenting on the personality and characteristics of an employee. There may be a list of criteria to check against such as behaviour, appearance, reliability and enthusiasm. The manager is asked to note the employee's ability to achieve targets.

Grading system: this is similar to the assessment review. The manager is given a list of categories to be assessed. This is done by selecting a grade which matches the employee's performance. Topics are related to employee effort, enthusiasm to begin and complete new tasks, the ability to work with others and qualities of leadership. This system may ask for a simple form of grading such as:

- Excellent
- Very Good
- Satisfactory
- Poor
- Very poor

Another type of grading system uses numerical scoring. A list of criteria is assessed by assigning points to each item. The points are added together and compared to a total potential score.

Disadvantages of grading and assessment: the main disadvantage of management assessment and grading is that they are subjective – there is little or no input from the employee. They are not sound techniques to define standards of performance, or to assess and address training needs for the employee.

Results-oriented appraisal: this is based on performance standards or specific targets. The manager and employee agree set targets which are relevant to the employee's job role, the department, and the organization as a whole. The targets or standards are set with a future incentive in mind. This may be a promotion, salary increase, or a transfer into another department.

In a results-oriented system the targets which are set may be quantitative (measurable) goals or qualitative (motivational) goals. A quantitative target is to increase productivity by 5 per cent, reduce budgetary costs by 10 per cent, or increase overall sales by 15 per cent.

A qualitative target is motivational and related to behaviour. For example, to effect better relations with trade customers, to create a spirit of teamwork in a small department, or to learn how to control a short temper.

> **Trainer's Tip**
> For more information on performance appraisals you can refer to the following publications:
> *The Personnel Manager's Factbook* (Knell, 1991)
> *A Handbook of Personnel Management Practice* (Armstrong, 1988)
> *Personnel Management, Theory and Practice* (Cole, 1988)
> *Personnel Management* (Attwood, 1989)

The Training Link to the Performance Appraisal

Training should be closely linked to the performance appraisal system in any organization. In most organizations, there is a formal system to review employee performance at least once a year. In training terms, the performance appraisal is a platform to identify:

- the requirements of new recruits
- inadequate performance by individual employees

- changes in organizational objectives
- the individual employee's goals for personal growth and development

The performance appraisal assesses individual employees in terms of their job performance. Training evaluates individual employees in terms of knowledge, skills and behaviour, and how they affect overall performance and the achievement of individual and organizational goals.

A performance appraisal is looking for results, where the role of training is to direct the process of achieving results. The final stage in the performance appraisal is the action plan to achieve targets. The appropriate action may require training to increase knowledge, improve skills or change behaviour.

The informal appraisal process

An informal appraisal is the continuous assessment of an individual's performance during the working year. This is where training can be helpful. The pre- and post-training meetings between manager and employee are useful appraisals of employee performance in terms of knowledge, skills and behaviour.

These briefing and debriefing sessions are a useful indicator of whether formal appraisal targets will be met. They assess the current and future potential of an employee, appraise training needs, and evaluate what needs have been met through training.

Who is Responsible for Co-ordinating Appraisal Data?

As head of training, it would be wise to compile regular reports which analyse the overall results of employee performance appraisals. This may be a personnel function. If it is your responsibility, you may wish to delegate the analysis of appraisals to a training administrator.

Post-training assessment

In terms of training, it is important to know the purpose for which managers are using the performance appraisal: either as a means of selecting training for individual employees, or as a method of post-training assessment, or both.

If you use performance appraisals as a method of assessing post-training performance, questions such as those provided in the checklist need to be answered:

CHECKLIST

1. How many individuals per course have achieved the training objectives?
2. What percentage of trainees have applied knowledge, skills or behaviour to the workplace as a result of training?
3. Which are the most successful courses in terms of achieving training objectives?
4. How have current levels of individual performance improved?
5. How have levels of organizational performance improved?
6. What training was of benefit to the individual but not to the organization?
7. What effect has training had on organizational profit?

Quantitative or qualitative analysis

The data gathered from performance appraisals can be subjected to analysis. We can state how the trainee's work has improved in terms of quantity or quality.

Quantitative: measurement is based on statistical analysis and can be substantiated in numerical terms. For example, due to technical training on the use of a new machine on a factory assembly line, an employee increased the number of products to be packaged per hour. Following training, job performance improved with a 5 per cent higher rate of packaging per day.

Qualitative: this type of analysis cannot be measured statistically. Instead, it offers insights into employee attitudes and behaviour patterns. It is a matter of observation and judgement to assess the quality of improved job performance.

Example

An employee was identified as displaying negative attitudes and a foul temper on the factory floor. Following a training needs analysis (TNA), the line manager suggested that he attend a personal development workshop to examine attitudes and behaviour. Although the employee was reluctant, he agreed to training after a personnel counselling session and a pre-course briefing with his line manager.

After training, the employee agreed to follow an action plan. The line manager noted, after an informal interview, that this particular worker's attitude to colleagues and management was beginning to change. He began to behave pleasantly on the shop floor and at staff meetings. Fewer complaints were lodged against him. The training was qualitatively assessed to have had a positive effect – on his attitude and behaviour at work.

The line manager followed up the interview with the regular performance appraisal later in the year. It was noted at the appraisal that the individual's productivity had increased due to a more positive attitude.

Conclusion

A performance appraisal is a means used to review performance standards and specific targets. As a formal review, it can be used to identify current job performance levels, and identify training and development needs.

Managers can use the performance appraisal system as a means of selecting training for individual employees and/or as a method of post-training assessment.

The data gathered from performance appraisals can be analysed either quantitatively or qualitatively.

▶ **CHAPTER REVIEW** ◀

1. A performance appraisal is a formal review of employee performance standards and specific targets.
2. The performance interview is concerned with:
   - setting targets or standards
   - measuring performance
   - planning the appropriate action
3. Training should be closely linked to the performance appraisal system in any organization.
4. The methods of reviewing performance are:
   - management assessment of the employee
   - grading or numerical system
   - results-oriented appraisal
5. The performance appraisal identifies:
   - the requirements of new recruits
   - inadequate performance by individual employees
   - any changes in organizational objectives
   - the individual employee's goals for personal growth and development
6. The responsibility of co-ordinating appraisal data may be a function of personnel and/or the head of training. There obviously needs to be co-operation and sharing of appraisal data between them.

19 Skills Necessary to Promote Training

> ## CHAPTER SUMMARY ◁

This chapter looks at what skills you need to promote training and to forge a link with other departments.
- A structured approach to training
- Promoting the benefits of training
- Developing effective communication skills
- Formulating training policy
- Developing proactive trainer roles

A Structured Approach to Training

A priority for any head of training is to promote training as an integral part of the personnel and management function.

A structured approach involves the assessment of training needs within the organization, the development of a training plan to close the gap between current performance and desired performance, and an evaluation of the outcomes of training. See Figure 19.1.

A structured approach to training is a means to:

- Increase employee commitment
- Enhance employee motivation
- Improve organizational performance
- Reduce costs and improve profitability

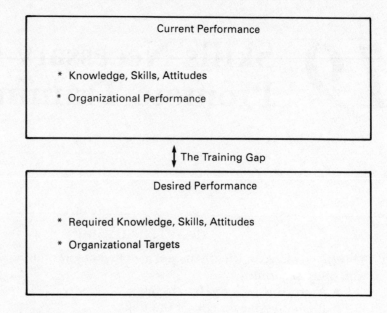

Figure 19.1 *The training gap*

To successfully communicate a structured approach we need to:

- Promote the benefits of training
- Develop effective communication skills
- Take active involvement in formulating the training policy
- Cultivate proactive trainer roles

Promoting the Benefits of Training

As head of training, it is your responsibility to promote the benefits of training to both management and individual employees. You need to determine what the attitude is to training within the organization, and establish what management and employees see as the benefits of training.

In Chapter 2, we discussed the organization's training mission. This clarified why the organization invests in training and what broad benefits can be anticipated from that investment.

General benefits to the organization

In any organization, the underlying benefits of a well-trained workforce are the ability to perform to a high standard at a more cost-effective rate. Specific benefits to be received from training are the ability to:

- Develop and sustain an adequate range of employee skills
- Foster staff knowledge and skills on a regular basis
- Enhance employee motivation
- Increase productivity
- Reinforce job performance
- Improve quality in the production of goods
- Achieve better quality of service to customers

General benefits to the individual

Individual employees gain enormously when the organization places an emphasis on training to develop the skills, attitudes, and potential of its workforce. Primary benefits for the individual are:

- The chance to develop personal knowledge and skills
- An increase in job satisfaction
- Greater expectations for internal promotion
- Longer-term career development
- Increased possibilities in the external job market

Activity

Your task is to promote the benefits of training which are specific to the needs of your organization and its employees.

1. Make a list of the benefits of training to your organization. List each of these benefits in order of priority.
2. Make a second list of the benefits of training relevant to each department within the organization. Place in order of priority.
3. Make a third list of benefits of training for the individual employees within your organization. Place these benefits in order of priority.

Developing Effective Communication Skills

In order to clearly explain the benefits of training to management and employees, you will require effective communication skills. Key techniques you will need to develop are:

- To behave in an assertive and proactive manner
- To demonstrate effective negotiation skills

Assertiveness skills

There are many experts on assertiveness today. One of the primary trainers in assertive behaviour is Rennie Fritchie. (*Working with Assertiveness*, BBC Enterprises, 1990). Fritchie defines an assertive person as someone who takes responsibility for their own behaviour, demonstrates self-respect and respect for others, is positive, listens, understands and tries to negotiate a workable compromise.

Takes responsibility for their own behaviour: assertiveness is basically a philosophy of personal responsibility. This means we are responsible for our own behaviour, and cannot blame another for our reaction to their behaviour. An intelligent response rather than instant reaction is vital for any trainer.

Demonstrates self-respect and respect for others: the essential ingredient of assertiveness is self-respect and respect for other people. If you do not respect yourself, who will? Self-respect for yourself as a trainer generates respect from your trainees.

Communicates effectively: the three principal qualities here are to speak honestly, openly and directly - but not at another's emotional expense. In other words, it means being able to say what you think or feel about an issue, without upsetting the person to whom you are speaking. It is essential that a trainer communicate effectively and directly with management and staff.

Demonstrates confidence and a positive attitude: to be assertive means developing self-confidence and a positive attitude. Self-confidence involves two factors: self-respect and knowing that we are well-trained to do our job and all that it entails. All trainers require enormous confidence and a positive attitude to handle the difficult situations which can arise in training.

Listens intelligently and understands: assertiveness requires intelligent listening and trying to understand another's point of view. We all think we are good listeners, but how often do we jump to assumptions when someone else is speaking, and how often do we interrupt to put across our point? A trainer requires skill in listening, and understanding a variety of issues and problems, in order to suggest positive solutions.

Negotiates and achieves workable compromises: the achievement of a workable compromise is very important to you as head of training. It is often needed to work out a situation which is acceptable to all parties concerned. The training department is often the key negotiator on behalf of several parties: senior management, trade associations, line management and employees.

Handles difficult situations with ease: assertiveness helps you to handle difficult situations with ease. It is not always easy to negotiate the training budget, to indicate the way forward for training in your organization, to persuade management of their role in planning training, and to manage the training function. Therefore, the ability to handle difficult situations assertively is a very useful skill.

> **Trainer's Tip**
> Behaviour can be classified into three simple categories: assertive, aggressive and submissive.
>
> *Assertive behaviour* (being honest, open and direct) is managing difficult situations with ease, saying the right thing in the right way, and feeling good about yourself and the outcome.
>
> *Aggressive behaviour* is displayed by blaming, showing contempt, attacking, patronizing, and insisting that your opinions are more important.
>
> *Submissive behaviour* is overly apologetic, too cautious to the point of timidity, being self-effacing and failing to communicate with confidence.
>
> The three types of behaviour are sometimes known as *tough, rough and fluff.*

Why is assertiveness important?

Being assertive ensures that you take up a more active role. For example: when promoting the role of training within the organization, proposing training policies and plans, negotiating a new budget or dealing with performance problems.

As head of training, you will need to be proactive – proposing ideas, indicating their purpose, promoting the benefits of training.

> **Trainer's Tip**
> Proactive behaviour is taking the initiative or instigating a course of action. This is the opposite to reactive behaviour which is simply responding to events or the actions of others.

Negotiation skills

Being assertive is the first step in effective communication, and is a great help in negotiation. In skilled negotiation, we are trying to achieve a win-win situation; i.e. both parties walk away having achieved something. This is called a workable compromise, and means both parties collaborate to resolve a situation. It does not mean that either side is compromised.

Example

The head of training in a local authority sought approval for a new training policy. The objectives were:

- To defend her proposed budget for a new training policy
- To prevent her budget being cut by the recommended 35 per cent
- To prepare and develop structured in-house training programmes for the new financial year
- To introduce a training needs analysis (TNA) to identify individual employee strengths and weaknesses
- To use the TNA to ensure that the new training programmes were designed with clear and realistic objectives

The training manager was already highly skilled in practical trainer qualities such as presentation skills and planning techniques. However, to successfully negotiate approval for the new training policy and its subsequent budget, discussions were held over two days with local councillors and the local authority's senior executives.

The training manager had developed a good assertive style. She listened to all the arguments and presented hers well. She took particular account of the financial constraints and staff problems presented to her by the chief executive officers.

Due to her clear assertive style, she was able to illustrate how she could begin to overcome these problems if the new training policy was accepted. She explained that if the policy was accepted, the training department would be able to relieve specific staff problems. In other words, she explained clearly the benefits of implementing the new training policy.

Finally, she indicated that she would be prepared to work with a reduced budget in order to make a start on developing structured training programmes. Even with a small training budget it would help to improve performance, to cut costs, and begin to develop a more efficient workforce.

Thus a workable compromise was achieved. Although the training budget was reduced by 15 per cent against the previous year's budget, the training manager demonstrated clearly how training represented a true financial investment for the authority. Her tactics were to:

- Draw a clear link between the proposed training activities and the local authority's financial constraints
- Indicate the problems which would continue to occur and develop if the new training policy was not acted upon
- Pinpoint the benefits to both staff and the organization if the new training policy was initiated
- Demonstrate a willingness to compromise on the budget

Activity
To evaluate how effective you and your team of trainers are in communicating the benefits of training, assess:
1. Which areas do you need to work in? Use the following list as a guide, but expand and add your own items to the list.
   - assertiveness skills
   - verbal communication skills
   - non-verbal communication skills
   - presentation skills
   - negotiation skills
2. What coaching or training is required to improve these skills?
3. What effect will these improvements have on the image and the influence of the training department?

Formulating Training Policy

Training policies play a major part in the achievement of organizational objectives. As a reminder, a training policy indicates what the organization is prepared to do in terms of training and developing its employees. In Chapter 3 we discussed the basic principles in setting training policies.

A training policy may stand on its own, or it may be linked to a range of organizational policies which deal with the management of human resources.

As a training manager, or head of the training function, it is vital that you are involved in the formulation of the organization's training policy.

CHECKLIST
1. Who is responsible for writing training policies and procedures in your organization?
2. How often is the training policy reviewed and rewritten?
3. What role do you play in formulating training policy within the organization?
4. How can you make a more significant contribution?
5. When is it decided that a training policy needs to be revised?
6. What is the best way to handle changes in the organization which affect the training policy?
7. What is the procedure for you to suggest the necessary changes to the organization's training policy?

Developing Proactive Trainer Roles

The reason for all training is to achieve organizational objectives. All training activities should be targeted to this goal. In order to do this, the training manager should play a proactive role.

To be proactive, we should first examine the theoretical roles of trainer expressed by R. Bennett (1988) and A.M. Pettigrew (in Harrison, 1991). (The practical aspects of the trainer's role are fully covered in Chapter 6).

Trainer roles have been analysed by many experts in the field of training and development. How do these roles relate to your particular job function?

Bennett and Pettigrew

Pettigrew's five trainer roles are: change agent, provider, passive provider, manager, and catalyst for transition. The five key roles expressed by Bennett are that of trainer, provider, consultant, manager and innovator.

Trainer: the trainer is primarily concerned with using a variety of methods to deliver training. In this role, the trainer acts principally as a facilitator and provides the necessary feedback to management as to how training objectives will be achieved.

Bennett	Pettigrew
Trainer	Passive Provider
Consultant	--
Innovator	Change Agent
Provider	Provider
Manager	Manager
--	Catalyst for transition

Pettigrew adds the role of catalyst; this is a transitional role when the trainer changes from reactive provider to proactive change agent. Bennett suggests one other key role, that of consultant.

Figure 19.2 *Trainer roles*

Provider: the provider has a more comprehensive role: this is to design and deliver training. However, there is the added responsibility of implementing a training needs analysis (TNA) to identify training objectives, and to provide training for trainers when required. This is a more proactive role. (According to Pettigrew, however, the role of provider is a reactive role as the trainer simply reacts to requests for training.)

Consultant: the consultancy role is linked to the training function. The consultant's role is to analyse current problems in the organization which involve personnel, and to recommend solutions that will resolve these problems through training. This role combines the proactive and reactive stance.

Manager: the manager's role is one of supervising, directing and co-ordinating the work of those involved in the training function. This role includes the development of training policies and training plans to complement corporate objectives.

The manager is responsible for the development, delivery, and evaluation of all training activities; the recruitment and training of trainers; and the control of the training budget. (Bennett's role of manager is not dissimilar to Pettigrew's role of training manager.)

Innovator: the innovator performs a highly proactive service by providing solutions to effect change and to solve performance problems.

This role dictates close involvement with top management and line management on organizational issues. Here the innovator advises management as to how training can make a successful contribution. (Pettigrew describes this role as that of change agent.) See Figure 19.2.

179

What influences your role as trainer?

Your role is dependent on many factors:

- The corporate culture in the organization
- The political environment
- Where personnel fits into the organization
- Where training fits into the personnel function
- Where training fits into the organization
- What the organization's commitment is to training
- The training department's influence on management
- The influence of technology on the organization
- The influence of new technology on training

The role of trainer is continually changing within an organization due to internal and external influences on the organization itself. For example, new technology, fashions and trends, the economic climate, and overall profitability of the organization all have a profound effect on its development. To be proactive, training must anticipate and respond to these changes.

Activity
1. Make a list of the key roles that you fulfil as head of training.
2. Have your team of trainers compile a similar list for themselves.
3. Note next to each role whether it is reactive or proactive.
4. Which roles should you and your team be providing?
5. What other contributions should you and your team make to the training function?
6. In which of Bennett's five roles do you and your team require training?
7. What steps should you be taking to provide these new roles?
8. When will you start?

How can you be proactive in improving the status and role of training?

To improve the status and role of training, we need to:

- Define the role of the training function within the organization
- Develop a structured approach to training
- Identify the key influences on training and trainers
- Establish all the required roles of trainer
- Build staff and management commitment to training
- Combat negative attitudes to training by promoting benefits

Conclusion

In this chapter we have examined how to be proactive in promoting the benefits of training, the importance of communication skills to accomplish this, the theoretical roles of trainer within the organization, what influences the role of trainer, and how to improve the status of training within the organization.

> ► **CHAPTER REVIEW** ◄

1. A structured approach to training is a means to:
   - increase employee commitment
   - enhance employee motivation
   - improve organizational performance
   - reduce costs and improve profitability
2. To communicate the importance of a structured approach to training you need to:
   - promote the benefits of training
   - develop effective communication skills
   - be actively involved in formulating training policies
   - develop proactive trainer roles
3. Training benefits the organization because it:
   - develops an adequate range of employee skills
   - regularly fosters staff knowledge and skills
   - enhances employee motivation
   - increases productivity
   - reinforces job performance
   - improves quality in the production of goods
   - achieves better quality of service to customers
4. The benefits of training to the individual are:
   - the chance to develop personal knowledge and skills
   - an increase in job satisfaction
   - greater expectations for promotion
   - long-term career development
   - external job possibilities
5. Bennett's general trainer roles are those of: trainer, provider, consultant, manager and innovator.

   Pettigrew's trainer roles are those of: change agent, provider, passive provider, manager, and catalyst for transition.
6. To improve the role of training requires certain steps:
   - to define the role of training
   - to develop a structured approach to training
   - to establish the role of trainer
   - to identify influences on the training function
   - to build commitment to training
   - to combat negative attitudes

20 Methods of Promoting Training

> CHAPTER SUMMARY ◁

We can build commitment to training and combat negative attitudes by promoting training effectively within the organization.
- Marketing training
- Promoting the training message
- Selecting the right method of communication

Marketing Training

Promoting training is an exercise in marketing. This is the process of matching our resources and capabilities to the needs of our client or customer. Marketing considers the wants and needs of the customer, then provides the required service or product.

In training terms, your customers are the organization's employees, and the training department provides training as a product (ie training programmes) and as a service (ie training needs analysis (TNA) and consultancy).

Trainer's Tip
An abbreviated definition of marketing is 'the management of customer demand'. In the case of training, our customers are those

> managers and staff within the organization whose training needs we must manage.
>
> Managing employee needs requires a proactive approach to training with the ability to promote the training message successfully.

The training message

If it is your responsibility to promote the training message, there are several ways to communicate resourcefully with senior management, line management and staff.

When writing on behalf of your training department, do so as if you were an ambassador for the whole organization.

Whatever method of communication you choose to promote the training message, it will include the following topics:

1. An analysis of the current role of training within the organization
2. How the training function contributes to the achievement of organizational objectives
3. Why training is an investment in the organization
4. How training assists in the development of personnel
5. Where training fits into the organization
6. Current training objectives and policies
7. Recommendations to improve or alter training policies
8. Why management should participate in the training process
9. Senior and line management responsibility for training
10. How management can be more involved in the training process
11. An appraisal of current trainer tasks and roles
12. Recommended new levels of responsibility for trainers
13. How employee and organizational performance will benefit from any recommended changes
14. Training programmes and timetables – internal & external

Promoting the Training Message

In many organizations there is little support for training at board level, or acknowledgement of how training can contribute to the achievement of corporate objectives. This lack of commitment to training often means that the organization's most valuable resource, people, is the least developed.

To improve the status of training within the organization requires a structured approach. This approach encompasses three important features:

1. To evaluate realistically the outcomes of training
2. To appraise the financial investment in training
3. To select the right method to promote training

Key tactics to promote the importance and value of training are:

- Meeting with senior management
- Strategic planning sessions
- Selection of the right method of communication

Meeting with senior management

The training manager should be proactive and effect a change in attitude at top levels of management. To promote change it is vital to attend senior management meetings, to recommend changes and to ask for decisions.

Senior management meetings are the appropriate forums to consult and brief senior management on training objectives, training policies and training plans.

To prepare for these meetings, establish which management meetings are the appropriate venue for training recommendations, how recommendations are presented, when decisions are taken and who authorizes training proposals. Other points for consideration are:

- The location and time for the meeting
- To determine who attends these meetings
- To establish the terms of reference for the meeting
- The agenda for the meeting
- Contributors at the meeting
- The format for recommendations and proposals
- What steps you must take to contribute
- How training can be included on the agenda
- How often the meeting should be attended by training management to gain credibility

---

Activity – The Functions of Management

There are five key management functions: leadership, strategic planning, development, control and communication.

The following steps will help identify which management functions are appropriate to you and your team of trainers.

---

1. Make a list of all the functions of management within your organization.
2. Make a list of all the current functions of training management.
3. Compare the two lists to determine which functions you and your training managers should be more actively involved in.

Strategic planning for training

The planning process is one of the most important aspects of management. Strategic planning is the move towards achieving your mission. It is the management process which links the development of corporate objectives to a realistic appraisal of your current resources.

In training terms, strategic planning is setting training objectives based on a realistic assessment of your organization's personnel and training needs. The key steps involved in the strategic planning process are:

- Secure commitment from key people
- Agree a timetable for action
- Confirm your training mission
- Undertake a situational analysis with a SWOT analysis
- Define your training objectives
- Establish who will develop the training plan
- Write the training plan
- Consult key people and revise the plan
- Implement the plan

Trainer's Tip – Implementing the Training Plan
The appropriate senior and line managers should be consulted and briefed at all stages. This may represent a collective team of managers from each department – including training and personnel. Refer to Chapter 5, The Training Plan.
Phase 1: All available training statistics and information should be collected, collated and analysed.
Phase 2: Organizational training objectives are clearly defined, and training policy and strategy are formulated.
Phase 3: Training policy and strategy are agreed by management and work is begun on developing the training plan.
Phase 4: The training plan is accepted by management.
Phase 5: The training plan is implemented.

Selecting the Right Method of Communication

The job has just begun once training objectives, policies and plans have been developed and authorized. Regular communication is essential to all senior managers, line managers and individual employees. The training manager should communicate:

- The benefits of training
- The functions of the training department
- Management responsibilities and participation in training
- Which training programmes are possible and when

Primary methods of communication are memoranda, reports, proposals, in-house newsletters, press releases and personal presentations. Correspondence is not as effective as face-to-face communication – ie personal presentation of a subject. However, correspondence offers an excellent way to communicate the value of training to management and staff.

One disadvantage of correspondence is that it can be ignored or mislaid. Therefore target the employee carefully – make sure that any written correspondence is relevant and useful to the receiver. This should help to ensure that your correspondence is read.

Memoranda

The main type of written communication, the memorandum, is quick, convenient and informal. Try to keep your message to one page and use it as a reminder, a written record of key decisions, or to confirm agreement of an issue. The memo is also a useful tool for brief pre- and post-training correspondence.

Receipt of a memo by a member of staff who does not normally receive correspondence can be a morale booster – its function is to keep the member of staff informed and motivate him/her at the same time.

Example – Memorandum

From:	Name	Date:
	(The Training Manager)	
To:	Name	
	(The Production Manager)	
Re:	Training action plan	

Dear Roy –

I would like to discuss your staff training needs with you. These have arisen as a result of the performance appraisals you held in your department last month.

This will assist us in planning the necessary training programme and budget for the new financial year.

I think that our meeting will last about one hour. Can you please let me know if any of the following days and times next week are convenient for you?

Monday,	12th October	10 am – 12 noon
Tuesday,	13th October	2 pm – 4 pm
Thursday,	15th October	1 pm – 3 pm
Friday,	16th October	2 pm – 4 pm

I look forward to seeing you.

Reports

The reasons for writing a report are to communicate complicated facts and opinions on a particular subject. Personal comment is valid as long as it is clearly distinguishable from other data in the report.

A training report may provide a useful account of current training activities, analysis of results, or simply a statement of progress.

Training reports should be brief and to the point, with data categorized in an easy-to-follow fashion. The material should be organized sensibly with tables and other data attached as appendices.

Report all facts clearly, write briefly and concisely, edit your material and discard irrelevant information.

Trainer's Tip
The following is a report outline:
1. Title Page with circulation list
2. Table of contents

One or two paragraphs each:
3. Introduction
4. Aims and objectives
5. Summary of key points
6. Methodology (method, order, arrangement)
7. Conclusions
8. Recommendations

Whatever number of pages are required:
9. Main report
10. Appendices or reference tables

Proposals

A training proposal recommends a plan of action and effectively promotes the training message. For example, to propose changes to current training, to put forward a new budget, to recommend changes to training policies, or to redefine training objectives.

The principal elements of a proposal are:

- Introduction
- Summary of contents
- The current situation
- Courses of action
- Full recommendations
- Conclusions

In-house newsletters

One excellent form of internal communication is the in-house newsletter. Whether it is used for your organization only, or is used in conjunction with other sister companies, the newsletter is a good method of communicating with employees throughout the organization.

A newsletter functions as an information service for the training department to communicate with all employees involved in training, personnel and management. It is also a useful platform for trainers to inform, persuade and discuss current training issues.

A newsletter can be used to:

- Praise the outstanding performance of employees who have benefited from training
- Publicize the latest training news
- Announce the recruitment of new trainers
- Highlight the addition of external trainers
- Explain the benefits of new training programmes
- Extol the value of the organization's training programme
- Write a regular column about the organization's training activities

The company newsletter is a superb medium for photographs with the relevant caption. Let's face it, we all enjoy a brief moment of glory!

Press releases

Every organization at some point oils its publicity machine to create news about personnel and training. If press releases are written and distributed, it is very important that employees are also kept informed.

Press releases can be posted on bulletin boards, and can also be sent to line managers and staff managers to be used as a briefing tool. In this way, all management and staff can participate. As a bonus, press releases are a useful tool to inform and motivate employees about the value and benefits of training.

> **Trainer's Tip**
> Ensure when writing press releases to keep them to one side of one A4 page. Each release should contain the following elements: Who, What, Why, Where, When and How.
> - Who is it about?
> - What is it about?
> - Why will it take place?
> - Where will it take place?
> - When will it happen?
> - How will it happen?

Personal presentation

Personal presentation is a very powerful means of promoting training. It provides an opportunity to allow for questions and discussion. Meetings where personal presentation can be used are:

- Board meetings
- Senior management meetings
- Staff meetings
- Departmental meetings
- Training and personnel briefings
- Formal and informal meetings

Presentations are a personal way to explain training programmes and activities to any size of audience. They can be used to brief management on new training plans and outcomes of training, or to communicate with staff about new training activities and how they will benefit.

Whether the presentation is made in the office, boardroom, meeting room or conference hall – it is an ideal stage from which to present training activities. A question-and-answer session (during or after the presentation) offers an opportunity to trainers to communicate the benefits and value of training first-hand, and to deal with any doubts or negative feelings which need to be aired.

We discussed in Chapter 19 the importance of assertiveness and the need to negotiate. These skills are essential to develop an effective presentation style. However, the most important technique in personal presentation is the ability to convince and persuade the audience of the value and benefits of training.

Presentations may be used effectively to promote the training message for any of the following:

- management meetings to discuss training objectives, policies or plans
- senior management meetings to discuss new training proposals
- staff meetings to present new training activities
- pre-training briefing sessions
- post-training follow-up meetings
- annual board meetings

Conclusion

To build commitment to training within the organization requires effective promotion of the training message. In practical terms, training managers are marketing training as a product or service to their clients, ie management and staff.

The value and benefits of training can be communicated to management and staff through written correspondence via a memorandum, report, proposal, newsletter or press release, or personal presentation at a meeting or conference. The method selected depends entirely on the objective and the message.

▶ **CHAPTER REVIEW** ◀

1. To promote training at any level requires a structured approach, to emphasize:
   - the right method to promote training
   - an appraisal of the financial investment in training
   - the outcomes of training
2. Correspondence and personal presentation are the major methods of communication to promote training. The most useful types of correspondence are:
   - memorandum
   - reports
   - proposals
   - in-house news letters
   - press releases
3. Personal presentation can be exercised at board meetings, senior management meetings, staff meetings, departmental meetings, training and personnel briefings, formal and informal presentation situations.
4. Presentations can cover many topics:
   - training objectives, policies and plans
   - new training proposals
   - new training activities
   - pre-training
   - post-training
   - annual board meetings

Glossary

Assertive
The behaviour of someone who takes responsibility for their own behaviour; demonstrates respect for others; and negotiates a workable compromise.

ASTD (American Society for Training and Development)
The American professional association for trainers.

Brainstorming
A practical exercise involving two or more people; brainstorming can produce a greater number of ideas than can be generated by an individual alone.

(CEUs) Continuing education units
American training and education standards set by the International Association for Continuing Education and Training in Washington D.C. It is not a regulatory body.

Corporate objectives
Corporate objectives reflect corporate philosophy. These are usually measurable short-term and long-term objectives which comprise the total range of a company's activities.

Cost-benefit analysis
A cost-benefit analysis compares the cost of training to the benefits expected to be received from training. Also used to evaluate the benefits of employing an external training consultant compared to the training costs incurred.

Course evaluation questionnaire
A questionniare used at the end of a training programme to obtain feedback from trainees.

Deliverer
A trainer who is essentially a presenter of training.

Discussive report
This type of report outlines topics for discussion, consideration or negotiation.

Evaluation
Evaluation assesses the total financial worth of training to the organization and the individual employee.

Explanatory report
Sets out a great amount of detail; can be used to examine a particular aspect of training which requires attention.

External trainers
External training providers or suppliers are often recruited to train in areas where internal trainers lack manpower, experience, expertise, time or credibility.

Facilitator
A trainer who enables participants to learn.

Financial statement
A means of organizing and presenting training accounts for the internal analysis of management.

Informative report
A brief, unbiased summary of the training situation; its purpose is to educate the reader about the background or history of a training circumstance.

Job description
A job description provides a basic framework for each individual's job, and outlines the key purpose, duties and responsibilities of the job.

Job specification
A job specification outlines the physical and mental activities demanded from the job. Essential characteristics of the job holder are outlined according to required knowledge, skills and attitudes.

Line management
In line management, there is a clear chain of command which directly links senior managers and line managers.

Motivation
The three main stages in the process of motivation are to identify an unsatisfied need; define the objective to satisfy the need; and take action to achieve the objective.

NCVQ (National Council for Vocational Qualifications)
The NCVQ publishes the criteria for national vocational qualifications; it is purely an accrediting body and does not issue certificates of qualification.

NVQs (national vocational qualifications)
Statements of competence in specific fields which have been introduced in many industrial and commercial sectors in the UK.

Open public course
Designed by an external training organization; the training is delivered at a venue of their choice.

Organization tree
The organization tree is a graphic representation of the formal relationship between functions, jobs and people in the company.

Performance appraisal
A formal process which measures current levels of individual performance, comparing them to past levels of performance.

Person specification
Each member of staff should have a person specification which briefly summarizes that individual's knowledge, skills, past experience and personal characteristics.

Personal goals statement
The personal goals which a training course is expected to fulfil for a trainee. Sometimes called an objectives statement.

Persuasive report
This presents an assessment of the training situation and recommends a specific course of action.

Post-training audit
A vital ingredient in the training appraisal process. Its purpose is to evaluate the effectiveness of training in terms of the trainee's application of knowledge, skills and behaviour.

Qualitative
Qualitative analysis cannot be measured statistically. Instead, it offers insights into employee attitudes and behaviour patterns.

Quantitative
Quantitative measurement is based on statistical analysis and can be substantiated in numerical terms.

Senior management
A manager at the most senior level within an organization, directly involved in the running of the company.

Staff management
A staff manager has responsibility over a number of staff, but is not responsible for the main operating activities of the organization.

SWOT analysis
A SWOT analysis helps to identify the internal and external factors which influence an organization. The SWOT matrix evaluates strengths, weaknesses, opportunities and threats.

Tailor-made training
Designed by an external training consultancy to suit a client's specific training needs.

Terms of reference
Identify what has to be done in terms of training; whose responsibility is the training function; and who is committed to and owns the training programmes.

Trainee statement
At the end of a training session, each trainee notes what benefits were personally gained from the training, and evaluates which training objectives were met.

Trainer competence levels
Trainer competence defines what knowledge, skills and attitudes are required by trainers, and what are their training needs.

Trainer consultant
A trainer working on special projects or as a problem solver within the organization. These activities usually have a link to training.

Training administrator
The training administrator relieves the trainer of organizational problems, and provides administrative support to the training department.

Training contract
The training contract reconciles the trainer's objectives for the training programme with those of individual trainees.

Training function
The four main stages of the training function are: identification and analysis of training needs; formulation of a training policy; implementation of the training; and assessment of training effectiveness.

Training mission
The training mission indicates the higher goals of the training department and should reflect the corporate mission.

Training need
A training need is usually defined as a gap – the gap between the requirements of a particular job and the capabilities of the employee currently holding the job.

Training objectives
The objectives of the training process which indicate how the training mission is to be achieved.

Training plan
A training plan describes the training methods to be used in delivering training within the organization, and translates training policy and strategy into tactics.

Training policy
A training policy states how training will achieve its set objectives, and spells out the focus of training activities within the organization.

Training strategies
A training strategy outlines in broad terms the campaign for the training function in any organization.

Transfer of learning
Evaluation of the trainee's performance and application of skills upon return to the working environment.

Validation
Validation is the practical measurement of a trainee's post-training job performance in the application of knowledge, skills and attitudes. There are two types of validation: internal and external.

Bibliography

Applegarth, M (1991) *How to Take a Training Audit*, Practical Trainer Series, Kogan Page, London/Pfeiffer & Co, San Diego.

Armstrong, M (1988), *A Handbook of Personnel Management Practice*, third edition, Kogan Page, London.

ASTD (American Society for Training and Development (1992) *Buyer's Guide Consultant's Directory*, ASTD, Alexandria, Virginia.

Attwood, M (1989) *Personnel Management*, Macmillan, London.

Back, K & K (1982) *Assertiveness at Work: A practical guide to handling awkward situations*, McGraw-Hill Book Company, London.

Bennett, R (1981) *Managing Personnel and Performance: An Alternative Approach*, Business Books Ltd, Hutchinson, London.

Bennett, R (ed) (1988) 'The Right Role' in *Improving Trainer Effectiveness*, Gower, Aldershot.

Bentley, T (1990) *The Business of Training*, McGraw-Hill Book Company (UK) Ltd, Maidenhead, Berkshire.

Bramley, P (1986) *Evaluation of Training, A Practical Guide*, BACIE, London.

Buckley, R and Caple, J (1990) *The Theory and Practice of Training*, Kogan Page, London/Pfeiffer & Co, San Diego.

Buckley, R & Caple, J (1991) *One-to-One Training and Coaching Skills*, Practical Trainer Series, Kogan Page, London/Pfeiffer & Co, San Diego.

Cole, GA (1988) *Personnel Management, Theory and Practice*, DP Publications Ltd, London.

Fletcher, S (1991a) *Designing Competence-Based Training*, Practical Trainer Series, Kogan Page, London/Pfeiffer & Co, San Diego.

Fletcher, S (1991b) *NVQs, Standards and Competence*, Kogan Page, London.

Fritchie, R (1990) *Working with Assertiveness*, BBC Training Videos, BBC Enterprises, London.

Garbutt, Professor D (1992) *Making Budgets Work, The Control and Use of the Budgetary Control Process*, Chartered Institute of Management Accountants, London.

Hackett, P (1990) *Success in Management: Personnel*, third edition, John Murray (Publishers) Ltd, London.

Hamblin, AC (1974) *Evaluation and Control of Training*, McGraw-Hill Book Company (UK) Ltd, Maidenhead, Berkshire.

Harrison, R (1991) *Training and Development*, Institute of Personnel Management, Wimbledon, London.

Herzberg, F (1975) *Work and the Nature of Man*, Crosby Lockwood, St. Albans

ITD, BACIE and Kogan Page (1992) *The Training Directory*, Kogan Page, London.

Johannsen, H & Page, GT (1990) *International Dictionary of Management*, Kogan Page, London.

Kirkpatrick, DL (1967) 'Evaluation of training', in *Training and Development Handbook* (eds Craig, RL and Bittel, LR) McGraw-Hill Book Company, New York.

Knell, A (Executive Ed) (1991) *The Personnel Manager's Factbook*, Gee, Professional Publishing Ltd, London.

Leigh, David (1991) *A Practical Approach to Group Training*, Practical Trainer Series, Kogan Page, London/Pfeiffer & Co, San Diego.

Maslow, AH (1970) *Motivation and Personality*, Second edition, Harper and Row, New York.

Meighan, M (1991) *How to Design and Deliver Induction Training Programmes*, Practical Trainer Series, Kogan Page, London.

Pettigrew, AM, Jones, GR & Reason, PW (1982) *Training and Development Roles in their Organizational Setting*, Manpower Services Commission, Sheffield.

Pont, T (1990) *Developing Effective Training Skills*, McGraw-Hill Book Company, London.

Rae, L (1990) *The Skills of Training, A Guide for Managers and Practitioners*, Gower, Aldershot.

Robinson, KR (1988), *A Handbook of Training Management*, revised second edition, Kogan Page, London.

Sharpe, R (1989) *Assert Yourself, How to Do a Good Deal Better With Others*, Kogan Page, London.

Stimson, N (1991) *How to Write and Prepare Training Materials*,

Practical Trainer Series, Kogan Page, London/Pfeiffer & Co, San Diego.

Vroom, VH (1964) *Work and Motivation*, Wiley, New York.

Vroom, VH and Deli, EL (1970) Management and Motivation, Penguin, Harmondsworth.

Weightman, J (1990) *Managing Human Resources*, Management Studies Series, (Series eds: Michael Armstrong and David Farnham), Institute of Personnel Management, Wimbledon, London.

Index